Nature's Lessons

Character Lessons from the World Around Us

Dennis Slone

VIP

VISION IMPRINTS PUBLISHING
A Thomas Nelson Company

www.thomasnelson.com

Tulsa, Oklahoma

NATURE'S LESSONS: CHARACTER LESSONS FROM
THE WORLD AROUND US
© 2006 by Dennis Slone

Published by Vision Imprints Publishing, Inc.
8801 S. Yale, Suite 410
Tulsa, OK 74137
918-493-1718

Original Printing: 7000

Unless otherwise noted, all Scripture quotations are
taken from the Holy Bible: New International Version,
copyright © 1960, 1962, 1963, 1968, 1971, 1972, 1973,
1975, 1977, 1995 by the Lockman Foundation. Used by
permission.

ISBN:1-599510-10-3
Library of Congress catalog card number:2005937642

Printed in the United States of America

Illustrations by Shelley Dieterichs Good Buddy Notes
151 West Argonne Avenue, 2nd Floor
Kirkwood, MO 63122
Phone: 866.GDB-UDDY or
Toll free: 866.432.8339
e-mail: shells@artbyshelley.com

Endorsements

"Dennis has written a book that challenged me to look at nature from a different perspective. The premise is that we can learn valuable character lessons by observing the world around us. I'll never look at glaciers the same after reading this book. They (glaciers) are like a modern-day Leonardo da Vinci patiently sculpting masterpieces for all to enjoy while, at the same time, offering us a great example of what can be accomplished through patience . . . Great read!"

—Brian Klemmer
Founder and CEO of Klemmer & Associates

"Dennis Slone is a family-oriented, God-loving man that has always amazed me with his knowledge and experience of nature. His passion comes to life in this divinely inspired composition."

—Rob Hubert

"Dennis is a modern-day Huck Finn. He is a servant leader that has clearly mastered the skill of observing the world around him while maintaining the curiosity and excitement of a child. His perceptions and insights into God's creation and his approach of tying character lessons to things from nature are unique, motivating, and inspiring. This book delivers a message that everyone should read."

—Dr. Tom Hill
Author, *Living at the Summit*
Co-Author upcoming *Chicken Soup for the Entrepreneurial Soul*

"I was inspired by Dennis' vision and character before he ever wrote *Nature's Lessons*. In this book I get a glimpse of the biblical principles that have laid the foundation for his success. May the world be drawn to Christ through these lessons."

—Brent Dearing
Financial Advisor at Renaissance Financial

"Dennis is a man of impeccable character. You can see the values that guide him sprinkled generously throughout this book. I highly recommend you get this book in front of every young person you care deeply about. The lessons learned will never grow old, never go out of style, and never fail."

—Dale Swain
Entrepreneur

"Fun, fascinating, and user-friendly! Dennis Slone has a unique gift of storytelling making it easy to understand and apply nature's lessons. Many thousands of lives will be positively transformed by the simplicity of the messages within his book."

—Bill Mayer
Author, *The Magic In Asking The Right Questions*

Contents

Acknowledgements
Introduction

CHAPTER 1
Ants and the Work Ethic
Learn the importance of a strong work ethic and
how it relates to leading a successful life.
13

CHAPTER 2
Horses Like to Run
Learn the value of exercise in leading
a healthy and active life.
23

CHAPTER 3
Eagles and Teamwork
Discover how much more can be
accomplished by working as a team.
33

CHAPTER 4
Otters Have Fun
Discover the importance of fun and why
we should include it in our lives.
43

CHAPTER 5
Family Life of Honeybees
Learn how to develop and maintain a
healthy family environment.
55

Chapter 6
Trees Seek Out the Light
Discover the importance of seeking truth
and following the path of integrity.
65

Chapter 7
Dogs and Loyalty
Discover the role loyalty has in
relationships with others.
73

Chapter 8
Bears Need Rest
Explore the importance of adequate
rest for a healthy life.
81

Chapter 9
Spiders and Creativity
Discover the importance of creativity and how to
make use of your talents.
89

Chapter 10
Flowers Are Charitable
Learn the importance of being
charitable to others.
97

Chapter 11
Patience of a Glacier
Discover the importance of patience in
leading a well balanced and harmonious life.
107

CHAPTER 12
Music and the Mockingbird
Discover the role of music in our lives.
115

CHAPTER 13
Geese and Encouragement
Learn the importance of encouragement and
support in living a happy and fulfilled life.
123

CHAPTER 14
The Persistence of Salmon
Discover how being persistent is essential
to realizing your dreams and goals.
131

Epilogue

Acknowledgements

This book is dedicated to my wife Tammy and children Chris, Denise, Angie, Kevin, and Megan. Without their love and support this book would not exist. God has truly blessed me with a wonderful family. I want to thank my parents Albert and Shirley Slone for teaching me God's word and training me to enjoy and learn from nature. I also want to thank my adopted parents, Paul George (P.G.) and Alice June (A.J.) Fiedler. They believed in me and saw talent that I never knew I possessed.

Special thanks to author and speaker, Brian Klemmer for his time, introductions and his training at Klemmer & Associates. Through this training I met several friends who were instrumental in helping me make this book a reality. They are Rita Norquist, Brian Zink, Bette Laughrun, Dyan Lucero, Carol Davidson, and Margie (Marvy) Fleischhauer. They held my feet to the fire and didn't allow me to perform at any other level except my best. I would also like to thank Rob Hubert who is an inspiration to me, a friend and a fellow companion on this journey called life.

Thanks to author and speaker, Bill Mayer. His coaching, ideas, and introductions were extremely helpful and instrumental in making this book a reality. From Bill I learned the power of asking big questions. I would also like to thank author and speaker, John Mason and his assistant, Denise Dietz of Vision Imprints Publishing for taking a chance on me and this book.

I would like to thank my editor, Patricia (Trish) Stelbrink, for her countless hours of instruction and insights. This book has been greatly improved by her attention to detail. She was patient with my deadlines and last minute requests. Additionally, I would like to thank my illustrator, Shelley Dieterichs, who worked with me in creating the perfect visual experience to accompany the text.

I would also like to thank the many who devoted time reading the original drafts of this text and offering input. In particular, I want to thank Cindy Gochenour for her feedback and insights.

Finally, I thank God for blessing me with the love of His word and creation. The beauty and wonder of His creation continually amazes me. I pray that others will be touched by His handy work as I have been.

Introduction

The idea for *Nature's Lessons* came after searching for the right topic for nearly ten years. I had started several books; however they did not capture the message that I wanted to relay to my children. Then one day, while preparing a study of the *Revelation*, the idea for this book came to me. I believe it was the answer to my prayers—literally. As I was poking through the Bible, I came across the following passage:

"For since the creation of the world God's invisible qualities—his eternal power and divine nature—have been clearly seen, being understood from what has been made, so that men are without excuse."
—Romans 1:20

From this verse, we are told that we can discern God's qualities, eternal power, and divine nature and that these things are clearly seen by observing what has been made—that is the universe. Stated another way, God reveals Himself through nature. All we need to do is look around us to observe His divine qualities, infinite power, and godly nature.

As I thought about this passage, it dawned on me that we could learn a great deal about living a successful, happy, and rewarding life by observing the world around us. The book that you are now reading is the result of this idea.

This book can be read from front to back or by choosing chapters at random. The character lessons covered in each chapter stand alone and are not dependent on any other chapter.

Each chapter covers a single character lesson that is tied to something in nature. Since God reveals His qualities in the environment, we need only look and marvel at the many examples that nature offers us. Good character and virtue are necessary for a well balanced, harmonious, and happy life. The entire Bible is a roadmap through this environment and is an owner's manual for human beings.

Every chapter begins with a passage from the Bible that corresponds with the character theme for that chapter. Within each chapter there is a discussion of a topic in nature and the lessons that can be learned by observing it. For example, in Chapter 6, *Trees Seek Out the Light*, light is defined as a physical phenomenon essential to trees and then as a mental phenomenon (truth) essential to us. Finally, a poem is added to the end of each chapter so that the lesson can be easily remembered.

You don't have to live in the country or a rural area to witness the marvel of God's creation. There are all kinds of plants and animals living in the most densely populated city. We need only open our eyes and look around us to witness the marvelous world that we inhabit.

If this book causes you to look at nature a little differently than before, it has achieved its purpose. If it increases your faith in God and causes you to dig deeper into His word, it has achieved its purpose. If it causes you to want to reach your true potential and lead a purpose driven life, it has achieved its purpose. If in some small way you look at the world around you differently than before, it has achieved its purpose.

Chapter 1

Ants and the Work Ethic

Go to the ant you sluggard;
consider its ways and be wise!
It has no commander, no overseer or ruler,
yet it stores its provisions
in the summer and gathers its food at harvest.
Proverbs 6:6-8

Work is most often associated with labor, effort, exertion, toil, and struggle. The word is used to refer to an occupation, job, employment, profession, or making a living. Webster's dictionary defines work as sustained physical or mental effort to overcome obstacles and achieve an objective or result. Work is a necessity of life in order to support our families, pay for college, buy our food and clothing, take vacations, and for many other things that we want to accomplish.

Work is also necessary to build strong, clean communities and churches, and to provide support for those less fortunate. We are called to serve God and, through work, demonstrate our faith. These type of works can be things that are not usually associated with effort, such as sitting and listening to a friend work through a difficult life issue like a death or terminal illness, visiting the sick and elderly, Christmas caroling, or praying fervently for someone's betterment.

We must all work in order to live. Maybe the best way to explore the importance of having a strong work ethic is by looking at the opposite character trait—laziness. Have you ever been around someone who was lazy? Have you ever been given an assignment as part of a team and someone on the team wouldn't pull their own weight? How does that make you feel? If you're like most people, it usually will make you frustrated or angry and you will begin to resent the slacker.

When I was 15 years old, I was putting up hay for a farmer in western Illinois. Hay is harvested from the fields several times throughout the spring, summer, and fall and either fed to cattle and horses or sold to others who do the same. The hay (and sometimes straw) is compressed into rectangular bails weighing 80 to 120 pounds with an approximate size of 1 ½ feet X 2 feet X 3 ½ feet. Our team that day consisted of two buckers and one stacker who rode on the wagon and stacked the bails for transport to the barn. For most of the day I was a bucker whose responsibility was to pick the bails out of the field and place (buck) the bails onto the wagon. In the beginning of a trip, when the wagon was empty, it was easy to put the hay on the wagon. Later, however, when the hay was stacked several bails high, it was difficult to throw the hay up to the stacker. I had the unfortunate circumstance of having a "lazy" teammate. I'll call him Alan. He was not the most energetic person I ever met. I spent most of the day bucking three bails for every one that Alan would pick up. By the end of the day, I was exhausted. We had bucked, stacked, and put 1,500 bails in the barn. Each of us would receive the same pay (5¢ a bail) for this effort which worked out to be approximately $75. Not bad for a teenager in the mid 1970s. Needless to say, I was not happy that my teammate Alan received the same amount of pay as I, but expended only a fraction of the effort.

After the farmer invited us to have a great meal with him and his wife, he paid us, fired Alan, and asked me to come back the next day. Alan was able to make money for the day on the backs of others. However, he was sent home and would never be invited back to work for this farmer again.

Laziness is often rewarded in the short-term like it was with Alan; however laziness is not a good long-term strategy for living a God-filled, abundant, and rewarding life. Aesop's fable of *The Ant and The Grasshopper* spells this out very well.

The Ant and the Grasshopper

In a field one summer's day a Grasshopper
was hopping about, chirping and singing to
its heart's content. An Ant passed by,
bearing along with great toil an ear of corn
he was taking to the nest.
"Why not come and chat with me," said the
Grasshopper, "instead of toiling and moiling
in that way?"
"I am helping to lay up food for the winter,"
said the Ant, "and recommend you
to do the same."
"Why bother about winter?"
said the Grasshopper.
"We have plenty of food at present."

The Ant went on its way and continued its toil. When the winter came, the Grasshopper had no food and found itself dying of hunger, while it saw the ants distributing corn and grain every day from the stores they had collected in the summer. Then the Grasshopper realized his error.

Moral
It is best to prepare for the days of necessity.

Let's look at the ant more closely. There are more than twenty thousand different species of ants and they live all over the world, with the exception of the coldest regions of the earth, like the Artic Circle. Ants are social insects and live in groups numbering from a few thousand to more than twenty million, such as the flesh eating driver ants in Africa. Some species build subterranean homes, burrowing ten to fifteen feet into the ground while others are nomadic and live their lives on the go.

A good example of the nomadic variety is the army ants of South America. Their homes consist of worker ants linking themselves together by means of special hooks on their legs, forming a living nest where the rest of the colony lives. Inside these living nests, the queen lays eggs, workers care and feed the young, and soldiers guard against intruders. Other army ants forage for food and, when they find it, they kill it, dissect it, and transport the booty back to the nest. There the worker ants distribute the food, feed the larvae, and carry off waste products. Each ant has a function to fulfill. The queen is the matriarch of the colony, laying upward of two thousand eggs a day and passing on the genetic material to future generations. Most of the eggs produced are worker ants, which perform the majority of the work in the colony. The remainder of the eggs turn into soldiers and a select few are reared to be breeding males and females that will leave the nest to form a new colony somewhere else.

All these ants within the colony share one thing in common: the survival of the colony. Each ant works single-mindedly filling its day with useful chores and duties. The ant doesn't have a boss or foreman; it doesn't wait for other ants to tell it what to do. Instead, without apparent guidance or direction, the ant busies itself with tasks that support the colony. It's as though the ant was born with an instinct for useful and purposeful duty. When the army ants decide to move to a new location (how they do this is still unknown), they all participate in the move. Workers collect all the eggs and larva and head off in the direction of their new home. Soldiers take up stations along the way to protect this promenade, brandishing their powerful jaws towards any intruder unlucky enough to wander into their path. Along the way, some of the workers act as bridges so that others can cross crevices and obstacles. When the whole colony reaches its destination, the workers take up their stations as either the walls or tunnels of the new nest or caretakers of the young brood living within. This whole procession happens with not a single ant shirking its duties.

Army ants are like the hunter-gatherers of the human world—not staying anyplace for an extended period of time. Another ant species that can be considered the farmers of the insect world is the leaf-cutter ants, or parasol ants, that are named after the chunks of leaves that they carry overhead back to the nest. The parade resembles a convoy of ants with umbrellas all headed for a Sunday afternoon picnic. The ants gather the leaves and other vegetation and chew them to pulp in specially prepared underground chambers. They regulate the conditions within their garden in order to raise a fungus that they use for food. Here in this colony workers divide their work into several main duties including gathering the leaves and vegetation, chewing the leaves into mulch, cultivating the fungus, removing waste, and caring for the young. Again, as with the army ants, there is no apparent ant in control. No boss or supervisor handing out work assignments and no manager watching over them to ensure they put in an honest days work.

As Proverbs so aptly says, we should look to the ant for wisdom as it relates to work. It prepares for the future and doesn't grumble or complain about its daily tasks. It does the work that we all aspire to by conquering the world around it. It takes on creatures many times its size and overcomes them. It's a victor on the battlefield of life and yet it doesn't shrink from taking out the garbage or changing the baby's diaper (or larvae's diaper in this case). It looks at the service that it performs, whether small or great, with the same determination and the same attitude. Its purpose in life is to serve.

As the Master has said, if we want to be a leader and become great, we must humble ourselves and serve others. We should consider our life and live it so that we can carry out our work to the best of our ability. Whatever work that we do should be approached with the highest sense of importance and duty. As an example, while taking out the garbage is not glamorous, it is necessary and important. If no one took out the garbage, we would soon be overrun with a rotting stinking mass of paper, plastic, and leftover food. Besides being unpleasant, it would be unhealthy and could possibly lead to disease and sickness.

What work do you do? How can you approach your work with an attitude of purpose and duty? Sit down and make a list of all the activities that make up your work. Your list might look like this:

- Take out the garbage
- Make the bed
- Clean my room
- Do my homework
- Feed and care for the dog
- Exercise
- Mow the lawn
- Rake the leaves
- Piano practice
- Employee at Mel's Restaurant

After creating the list go over each item listed and ask yourself how you can do it better, faster, cheaper, or make it less burdensome. For example, let's look at mowing the lawn. What is your attitude when it is time to cut the grass? Do you enjoy the time outside in the sun or do you dread the hot summer days? Do you look forward to the exercise or do you hate to sweat? What would happen if you didn't cut the grass? How tall would it get? Would your dog be able to go outside without getting covered in fleas, ticks, and chiggers? Would flowers and plants that you want to grow survive in tall weeds? Snakes love tall grass. Let's suppose you dislike cutting the grass. Instead of thinking about cutting the lawn as work, think of yourself as a sculptor that is creating a masterpiece. Now your work becomes art and you become the artist. Instead of cutting corners and leaving some grass uncut, you trim away all excess to reveal a beautiful yard. Make a list of all the benefits of cutting the grass and doing your work to the best of your abilities. Your list may look like this:

- I feel good about myself.
- The exercise is good for me.
- The lawn looks great.
- The value of this property increases.
- Birds can eat harmful insects when the grass is short.
- My dog can run freely without getting fleas, ticks, and chiggers.
- I'm following the example of Proverbs.
- I contributed to the welfare of the family.
- I earned money (if you get paid for it).
- The flowers can grow without getting choked out by weeds.

You can create a benefits list for each of the items listed in your work list. If some of the items are burdensome, think of ways to make it easier or less strenuous. Add these to your benefits list. Approach each task as though you are working for God directly.

"And whatever you do, whether in word or deed, do it all in the name of the Lord Jesus, giving thanks to God the Father through him."
—Colossians 3:17

You are working for God in all you do and serving others as a result. No task is too small for God; therefore, there are no tasks too small for you.

Finally, go into your yard or neighborhood park, find an ant colony and observe them for awhile. Take a notebook and write down what you see. How do the ants find a discarded piece of candy? After one finds it, how long does it take before many others show up to help carry it home? What can you learn from the humble ant? Compare the ant to the grasshopper. What differences do you see? Is Aesop's fable accurate?

Diligent and purposeful work is rewarding. It helps us feel good about ourselves and we will receive big rewards in the long run. Just as the farmer was watching me when I was putting up hay for him and rewarded me by paying me and retaining me for another day, so will our Father in heaven reward you for faithfully and diligently doing the work He has set before you. Happily, when the winter of life has come, you will be prepared, like the ant, to face whatever challenges are put before you.

Follow the ants to see where they go,
For there is wisdom to find in their daily flow.
They work from early dawn 'till after sunset,
And if we follow their example, we'll have no regret.

Chapter 2

Horses Like
to Run

*Don't you know that you yourselves are God's
temple and that God's spirit lives in you?*
1 Corinthians 3:16

Exercise is very important to our health. It helps us relieve stress, ward off diseases, lose weight, and feel better. We should take every opportunity to exercise. Exercise has been shown to extend our lives and increase the number of years we live both healthy and active lives. It makes us feel good about ourselves and, as a result, we are more attractive to others. Exercise helps eliminate harmful toxins and increases bone and muscle strength. In short, exercise helps the whole body.

How important is our body? Let's see what Paul wrote to the Christians at Corinth:

"Do you not know that your body is a temple of the Holy Spirit, who is in you, whom you have received from God? You are not your own; you were bought at a price. Therefore honor God with your body."
—1 Corinthians 6:19-20

Again, the Psalmist says:

"I praise you because I am fearfully
and wonderfully made."
—Psalm 139:14

Our bodies are made up of trillions of cells—
estimates range from fifty to over one hundred tril-
lion. We have miles of blood vessels and nerve fibers
running through our bodies. Our eyes are a techno-
logical wonder. The cells that perceive light on the
retina are replaced every ten days and manipulate
the images we see long before sending them on to
our brains. Our bodies can be controlled so gracefully that they can etch out a beautiful pattern on ice
using a pair of skates or dance a ballet that will
bring tears to even the most reticent person. We
have been made in the likeness of the Eternal One.
We are truly wonderfully made.

Realizing that our bodies are a temple and
that we are made in the likeness of God, we need to
care for and properly maintain them. Sadly today, at
least in the western culture, many have grown up
with habits that are not suited for maintaining long-
term health. Deaths caused by degenerative
diseases are on the rise. Diseases such as cancer,
heart disease, diabetes, and osteoporosis are caused
by poor diet and lack of exercise. The rate of childhood obesity is on the rise. Convenience foods, often
loaded with empty calories (very little nutritional
value) are eaten in place of whole foods, such as lean
meats, fresh fruits and vegetables, and whole
grains. This has reached nearly epidemic propor-
tions. To make matters worse, we (at least in the
United States) are taking more medications than at

any other time in history. These medications often only treat the symptoms and do nothing to solve the root of the problem. These medicines often have their own side effects, and may, over the long-term, be worse than the original condition. What should we do to care for and maintain our bodies? Before we answer this question, let's take a close look at the horse.

Horses love to run. They are similar to us in that they sweat when they get hot. Most animals do not sweat and they can overheat if they overexert themselves. Horses have been known to run for more than twenty miles straight. Of course humans can do the same—at least those in good physical condition.

Horses not only like to run (some might say they were born to run), they like to work too. Big draft horses, like Belgians, Clydesdales, and Percherons, are very strong. They have been used for thousands of years to work for us. They have been used on treadmills (though oxen are more favored for this task), pulling wagons and chariots, plowing fields, pulling felled timber from the deep woods, and many other tasks that are too burdensome for man. Even today horses are used extensively in the Amish and Mennonite communities for all types of farm work. As a side benefit, their manure can be used to fertilize gardens and crops.

Horses are some of the most expensive animals available for purchase. Some pure racing horses can fetch millions on the open market. In fact, a champion stallion can earn his keep by breeding other animals for thousands or hundreds of thousands of dollars for each foal produced.

We can learn much from our companions—the horse. They can be as loyal as a dog and make very good pets. The main lesson we can learn from them is the love of exercise. Wild mustangs can and do run across the dry canyon lands of the southwest United States. They run and kick just for the pure enjoyment of having the breeze blow through their mane. This running builds strength and helps them to defend against predators, such as mountain lions or coyotes.

If you look closely at a horse, you will see a body that is sculptured in muscle. They are very powerful animals. They can run up to speeds of twenty-five miles per hour, pull logs up steep terrain, haul hundreds of pounds of supplies over great distances, and pull a plow through heavy clay soil.

Horses come in all shapes and sizes. Some are very small like the pygmy horses; pygmy horses have been used as an alternative to dogs for some people who suffer from mobility problems. Others are very large like the Belgian. Some make very good riding horses like the Tennessee walking horse or the Rocky Mountain saddle horse. Others make good pets, such as the Shetland pony; however they are not the most comfortable horse to ride.

As an aside, I used to ride a Shetland pony when I was ten or twelve years old. My step-grandfather and my cousins owned these ponies. There was one particular pony that was ornery. It apparently didn't want us (or at least me) to ride him. When I would ride him, he would head straight for an embankment and suddenly stop when he crested it throwing me headlong down the hill.

Sometimes horses have been crossed with their cousins the donkey. This cross breeding yields an animal called a mule. Mules have very good endurance, better than a horse (which they get from the donkey), and have good strength (which they get from the horse). Mules have been used for farming, pulling wagons, and general utility. They are best suited where the climate is dry. Many miners found that mules were essential for carrying supplies to mining camps in the mountains. Whole mule trains were put together for taking large quantities of supplies to remote locations. The mule requires less water and food than a horse, however they have more endurance.

Exercise keeps the horse healthy. Horses kept in stables and that are not frequently exercised, tend to suffer more ailments and do not live as long as the old roan that is allowed to run freely in the pasture.

When we look closely at horses and their crossbred cousins, the mule, we see examples of what we should do in our own lives. God has shown His qualities in all creation and there are many lessons to be learned from the horse. One very important lesson is working our bodies physically. This can yield huge benefits for us in the long run. Exercise has been shown to prevent heart disease and cancer, reduce obesity, build strength, reduce stress, increase mental alertness, and make us feel better.

A good example of someone who was very sickly as a child and became strong through bodily exercise is Teddy Roosevelt, our 22nd president. He was often bed ridden when he was young and suffered all kinds of allergies and sicknesses. He was thin and frail. He eventually found a love of riding horses and exploring the great outdoors. Through this, he became known as a very strong and brave man. He led a group of calvary in battle up San Juan Hill to victory over the Spanish. He became a war hero and was eventually elected president.

Another example is Wilma Rudolph. Born prematurely in 1940, she suffered all types of ailments in her early childhood including measles, mumps, scarlet fever, chicken pox, pneumonia, and polio. The doctor told her mother that she would never walk. Her parents and siblings (twenty-one of them!) encouraged her and helped her walk with the aid of a metal brace. Over time she was able to walk without aid and, at the age of twelve, decided to become an athlete. She went on to win a bronze medal in the 1956 Olympics and three gold medals in the 1960 Olympics—all in running events!

Starting any exercise program can be difficult and sometimes we put it off because we have other things we want to do. A few years ago, I owned a Tennessee walking horse called Star. I loved her and she loved me. She was a jealous horse and would push others away from me—even my wife and dog. We got along great until I would ride her. At first, Star would act like her front leg was hurt. If that didn't work, she would head for the pine trees and try to knock me off her back. When that didn't work, she gave up and we would have a great ride. She finally quit doing this to me; however she would do it to others when they tried to ride her. She was reluctant to exercise at first, but then she enjoyed it after she finally started.

We are really no different. How many people set New Year resolutions to start exercising? They even go to their local gym and sign up for a year—often costing hundreds of dollars. The first day to the gym they are usually enthusiastic; after a few trips to the gym, the newness wears off and drudgery sets in. Within three weeks of signing up, the majority never return for the remainder of the year. They end up subsidizing those few who take their health seriously. There are many who like to portray to the world that they belong to a gym; however they don't want to do what it takes to maintain healthy and strong bodies.

Are you one of the subsidized or are you one of the subsidizers? If you are someone who believes that your body is a temple, then exercising is necessary.

So, what types of exercise should we do? Exercise can take many forms such as running (like horses), weight lifting, mountain climbing, skiing, hiking, swimming, dancing, and playing sports. Thousands race in marathons (twenty-six miles) each year. The exercise program we choose should fit our lifestyle, our current health, and should be something that is enjoyable. If exercise is work or drudgery, then it will be difficult to maintain over the long haul.

When we are active our bodies strengthen themselves. Our bones, muscles, cartilage, and ligaments all get stronger. This decreases our chances of injury, such as breaking bones, pulling or tearing muscles, or pulling bones out of sockets. Exercise also increases our ability to fight germs. As a result of exercising, we take in and excrete larger amounts of fluids. This helps to rid our bodies of waste products and speeds healing.

There are many spiritual benefits as well. We usually feel much happier when we exercise and this can put us in a better mood. If we are in a better mood, we will be more patient, kind, caring, and tolerant of other people. This has the added benefit of causing others to want to be around us. Many will want to emulate us as well. Hence, we become good examples and mentors for others to follow.

Many times we can feel lazy or tired and will put off exercising. Sometimes this is okay. Our bodies often give us clues as to what we should do. However, we shouldn't put off exercise for too long. It takes only a few days to start losing the strength and stamina that we have worked so hard to attain. The nice thing, though, is that we can get back into shape very quickly if we haven't laid off too long. We need rest, too (see Chapter 8, *Bears Need Rest*).

So when and how can you get started on a life long program of regular exercise? First, if you have any health condition, see a doctor before starting any regimen. Also, some forms of exercise are inappropriate for young ages. An example is weight training (especially heavy weight training). Bones of young folks, ages twelve and under, have not completed growing and can be deformed if put under too much stress. This was seen in Great Britain before they introduced child labor laws. Children were often pushed to do heavy labor that would be difficult for an adult. Over time their bones were deformed because of the heavy stress. Fingers were often crooked and backs slumped because of repetitive work or heavy lifting. So caution must be taken not to over stress the body when you are young.

The best programs should include things that you enjoy doing (or you enjoy the results). If you do not enjoy doing it, it will be difficult to maintain over time. An example would be, if you enjoy walking in the woods, then take regular walks in a park or some other area where you are allowed access. Do this regularly, such as every other day. Make the walk strenuous enough that you increase your heart rate to approximately 90 to 120 beats per minute. This will strengthen your heart and muscles. In addition, you can enjoy the scenery around you and take in the sights, sounds, smells, and textures (feel the bark on the trees or the leaves crunching under foot).

Take a trip to see a horse show or go to a local farm where you can watch horses in action. If you live close to a Mennonite or Amish community, take a day and watch them work their horses. Observe how the horses behave. They love to run and pull in the harness. Are there opportunities in your life that you can mimic the horse and do something manually? For instance, take the stairs instead of the elevator. Cut the grass with a push mower instead of riding mower. If you live close to your grocer, ride a bike or walk instead of taking a bus, cab, or car. Your body is a temple that houses the spirit of God. Treat it with the respect that it deserves.

❧

Run like a horse with the wind in its mane,
Gallop through life across the dusty plain.
You are blessed with a temple fearfully made,
So run like a horse through the grassy glade.

Chapter 3

Eagles and Teamwork

Even youths grow tired and weary, and young men stumble and fall; but those who hope in the lord will renew their strength. They will soar on wings like eagles; they will run and not grow weary, they will walk and not be faint.
Isaiah 40:30-31

In a land where the spirit of rugged individualism is celebrated, teamwork is often not given the attention it needs. Even in the day of the pioneer, when rugged individualism was king, people did not conquer the great West by themselves. Instead, they depended on supplies from the east, military outposts (forts) for protection, and the train for transport of beef and other farm products to the east. All these take teamwork; often by people who don't even know each other.

Webster's dictionary defines teamwork as work done by a number of associates each doing a part, but all subordinating personal prominence to the efficiency of the whole. The definition sounds clinical. To paraphrase, teamwork is working together to achieve a common goal or objective. Quite possibly, without teamwork, man would still be living in caves struggling to find enough food to survive. Nothing of significance would have been built. Think of the seven great manmade wonders of the ancient world:

- The Hanging Gardens of Babylon
- The Lighthouse of Alexandria
- The Statue of Zeus at Olympia
- The Great Pyramid of Giza
- The Colossus of Rhodes
- The Mausoleum at Halicarnassus
- The Temple of Artemis Ephesus

None of these great wonders would have existed were it not for people working together as a team towards a common goal. One person can have a vision; however if the vision is large and touches many lives, that person will need a team to carry it out and make the vision real. Even as I write this book, I don't create it alone. For instance, the information for the seven wonders of the ancient world was gathered by other people and put into books and on Web sites for others to read and understand. I'm writing the words; however I have a team of people helping me. My wife, Tammy and my two oldest daughters proofread. My editor helps me clarify, correct grammar, and offers improvements. An artist illustrates it. Others will print it and still another group of people will distribute it. We are all working together as a team to make it real.

Let's consider the effect of teamwork on The Great Pyramid of Giza. It's generally accepted that the pharaoh Khufu had the pyramid built as a monument and temple to be used as his tomb when he died. The pyramid was built over 4,500 years ago and is a popular tourist destination today. Construction took place over a period of 20 years using two ton stones. There are no records on the construction technique used to build the pyramid; however it is a marvel that it was built without the benefit of modern machinery and tools. Until approximately 200 years ago, the great pyramid was the tallest manmade structure in the world.

Let's assume the pharaoh had the vision to create the great pyramid. We don't know as to whether it was his idea or whether someone else thought of it and he decided to build it, so we'll give him the credit. However, it would have been an idea forever if he hadn't had a team to create it. The stones were quarried some distance from the pyramid and had to be transported to the location. For this, the pharaoh would need stone masons, carpenters (for building boats and wheels), rope makers, tool makers, and potters (for making vessels to hold and transport water and food). Once the stones were on site, architects and engineers would be necessary to guide the placement of the stones. A host of support people would be necessary to provide for the basic needs of all the workers. The support people would provide food, water, materials for shelter, clothing, and medicine. Indeed, the area around the great pyramid would have been a hive of activity during the construction of the pharaoh's temple. Once the inner chambers were complete, artists and scribes would have painted and written the story that Khufu wanted recorded. Goldsmiths and potters would have busied themselves making vessels and instruments for the king to enjoy in his afterlife. The Egyptians believed in life after death and they had to prepare for this journey by filling their burial chamber with things they would need once they completed their destination. Items often included food, clothing, weapons, and even the family pet. Without teamwork the pyramid would not exist today.

Another great example of teamwork is the Roman coliseum and water aqueduct system. These great structures are truly a testament to Roman architecture and engineering. The coliseum was built in 80 AD and took ten years to build. The aqueducts were built over a period of five hundred years and supplied the Romans with endless water supply for bathing, drinking, and water fountains.

The coliseum is located in Rome, Italy and could hold up to fifty thousand spectators. This was the Roman equivalent of our modern day circus, television, and theatre all wrapped in one. Roman citizens came to see exotic animals perform, gladiators fight to the death, and even mock naval battles. It is four stories tall and has eighty entrances. Again, as was the case with the great pyramid, a whole team of people were needed to build this structure. Architects, engineers, stone masons, carpenters, metal smiths, weavers, and a host of other people were needed to act as a team focused on building this great structure. While it may have been the idea of a single individual, it took literally thousands of people to make it real.

The aqueduct system that fed Rome consisted of eleven conduits bringing water from the hills surrounding the city. The longest was over fifty-seven miles long. The Romans tunneled through hills, crossed valleys, and bridged hollows using stone as their material of choice. Some of these aqueducts are still in use today. They use the force of gravity to get the water to flow gently from the source to holding tanks in the city. Many artisans of all trades were necessary to build these great marvels.

In all these cases, a team of people were needed to accomplish the tasks. Each person on the team has to do their part in order for the objectives to be realized. Perhaps one of the most interesting things about these teams is that no single person possessed all the skills or ability to create any of these impressive structures. This is true of most teams. The exception is very small teams that conduct simple tasks. A great example of teamwork is multilevel marketing where teams of people work together to sell products and services by building relationships with their customers.

Let's turn our attention to nature for an example of teamwork. Eagles are associated with all sorts of things like freedom, great hunting ability, and even valor; however few think of them as great team players. They are. Eagles work together to raise their young and ensure the survival of their species. They work together building impressive nests and supplying food for their hungry young.

There are many species of eagle; however, we are going to consider the bald eagle. The bald eagle mates for life and can live up to fifty years old in captivity. They will only mate with another eagle if their lifetime partner dies. The normal lifespan for an eagle in the wild is approximately thirty years. Eagles mature at about five years old and develop their characteristic coloring of white head and dark body by this age. Prior to age five, their feathers range from a mottled mixture of brown and white to dark brown.

When an eagle finds a mate they establish their bond through an elaborate acrobatic courtship. They will pursue one another through the air, either soaring gracefully or diving after each other reminiscent of a World War I dogfight. During the dives they will lock talons and cartwheel end over end until they get close to the ground. Once near the ground, they release their grip and climb up to the clouds and do it all over again.

Once they have established their bond (I call it eagle marriage), they look for a suitable site to build their nest. They prefer cliffs, overhangs, and tall trees where they have an unobstructed flight path. Eagles are not like owls and other forest birds that can maneuver through trees and limbs. They need a clear path for take off and landing. Most nesting sites are located near rivers, lakes, and along costal waterways.

With the site chosen, the nest building begins. Eagles use limbs as large as six feet long and two inches in diameter to construct their nest. The female is larger than the male and regularly takes over the task of actual construction while the male searches for building materials. They use all types of materials including branches, leaves, pine needles, and grass. Eagles regularly collect other things and put them in their nest like soda cans, balls, light bulbs, and bits of cloth. No one is sure why they do this, but it does make for an interesting structure.

Eagles return year after year to the same nesting site. Each year the eagles expand on their nests until they sometimes become large enough to topple a tree. The largest nest recorded weighed over two tons, was nearly ten feet in diameter, and was twenty feet deep. Some nests have been occupied by the same eagles for over forty years.

When the nest is ready, the female will lay one to three eggs. Each egg is approximately twice as big as an average chicken egg. Both the male and female will take turns incubating the eggs while the other hunts or watches from a nearby perch, although the female spends more time on the nest. After a thirty-two day incubation period, the eggs hatch. The eggs do not hatch all at once, but usually within a few days of each other.

Once hatched, the young eaglets have a voracious appetite and grow quickly. Eaglets can grow up to six ounces a day. The mother and father work together to feed their young. They don't regurgitate their food like other birds, but bring the kill to the nest and tear off chunks for the eaglets. When the eaglets get old enough and strong enough to tear the meat themselves, the mother and father no longer feed them. They still bring the kill to the nest; however they don't tear it into chunks for them. This behavior is repeated when it's time for them to fly. Mother and father will sometimes quit feeding them in the nest so that they have to fly to a nearby perch to eat.

Through teamwork and dedication a pair of eagles can build nests many times their size, raise young, and look out for one another. Teamwork is as essential to the eagle as it was to the Egyptians and the Romans. Just as the Egyptians and Romans used people with specialized skills to build their pyramids, aqueducts, and coliseums, so too, does the eagle. The female takes primary responsibility for the construction of the nest, while the male takes primary responsibility for gathering the building materials. Each shares nesting duties so that the other can hunt for food. Both eagles help feed their young eaglets until the eaglets are large enough to leave the nest.

We've seen how teamwork is essential for the eagle, so how is it important to us? And how can we become better team players? First, teamwork is indispensable in our daily lives. Let's consider a marriage between a husband and wife. Without teamwork and cooperation, they cannot expect to provide a safe, loving, and encouraging home. If each person is only interested in what they want and not what is best for the marriage, then their relationship will soon be in trouble.

Let's consider another example: Think of a softball team where a player's performance directly impacts the performance of the team (whether the team wins or loses or plays the best they can with the talent available). Let's further assume that the player is the first basemen and the player doesn't practice or half-heartedly plays the game. What are the chances that they will drop a ball thrown to them? Or, worse yet, miss an entire play because the player wasn't paying attention? Not only does this affect the player, but also everyone else on their team and the opposing team. Yes, I said opposing team. If by their mistake the player allows the other team to win, they will be cheated of a true victory! If a player plays their best and loses, everybody wins (they may lose the game and still win inside because they did their best). If a player plays half-heartedly, everybody loses. This holds true for everything you do.

Be a team player in sports, at work, at church, in your family, even when you are alone—because you're never alone. The Master is always your teammate and is with you always; even unto the ends of the earth.

". . . And surely I am with you always,
to the very end of the age."
—Matthew 28:20

When I was in high school my senior year we had good talent on our football team and had the chance to have a winning season. However, there were only a few of us on the team that took football seriously and wanted to do our best. We never missed a practice and trained hard. We ended up with a 4-5 losing season because many on the team were not focused on giving their best. We had excellent talent on the team, but we weren't dedicated and didn't apply ourselves. It was disappointing. When I graduated, I made a vow that I wouldn't join another team that was not prepared to do their best. I haven't to this day.

Think of some ways that you can perform as a better team player. Make a list of three areas in your life where you can give your all as part of a team. Your list may look something like this:

- I want to be a better team player in my family.
- I want to be a better team player on my sports team.
- I want to be a better team player in my Bible study group.
- I want to be a better team player at my job.
- I want to be a better team player in my studies (classroom, if at school, or parent, if home schooled).

- I want to be a better team player in my friendships with others.
- I want to be a better team player in my church.
- I want to be a better team player in my community.

If you are fortunate enough to live close to where bald eagles nest, then take some binoculars and spend some time watching them. What can you learn from the eagle? If you don't have access to this marvelous creature, then take a trip to the zoo and observe them in captivity. You can also look them up on the internet or check out a book from the library. Enjoy the majestic bird and put teamwork into your life. Who knows what you will be able to accomplish with the assistance of others.

Eagles soar in the heavens with outstretched wing,
Watching them fly causes my soul to sing.
Teamwork is a character that eagles share,
No task is too large, if only we dare.

Chapter 4

Otters Have Fun

Command those who are rich in this present world not to be arrogant nor to put their hope in wealth, which is so uncertain, but to put their hope in God, who richly provides us with everything for our enjoyment.
1 Timothy 6:17

When the word fun is mentioned, what comes to mind? Enjoyment? Doing something pleasurable? Acting carefree? Laughter or exhilaration? Or do you feel guilty or irresponsible?

Having fun is necessary to living a well-balanced life. The old saying is true, "All work and no play makes Jack a dull boy." God expects us to enjoy ourselves. There are many references in the Bible that talk about singing, dancing, and being merry. Serving God is a joyful experience. While it is not possible to be joyful all the time, the more enjoyment we choose to experience, the more of a positive impact we will have on those around us.

Too often Christians and pious people live their lives in drudgery with smug faces and martyr personalities. Many early settlers of the United States were cut from this cloth. They believed their lives were to be lived out in toil and pain in the hopes that, by living such a life, one would enter into eternal rest. How they arrived at this presumption is a discussion for another time; however they became morose and stilted as a result of this belief. It is almost as though they believed that by living in misery, they could atone for mistakes they made. Unfortunately, many today believe this and miss the boundless joy that surrounds us every day.

While I'll be the first to admit that there is a time and place for a stoic attitude, we are not to live our lives like a robot. Having fun or enjoying ourselves is necessary for us to recharge our batteries and is essential to a balanced life. Our brains release chemicals, such as endorphins and serotonin, which make us feel good and bring us a sense of peace. In turn, we live longer and more abundant lives. Studies have shown that laughter and joy help heal sickness and speed recovery. Think of a time when you laughed for an extended period of time. How did you feel? If you are like most people, you felt very good.

Enjoyment can be experienced through activities we normally associate with pleasure, such as playing baseball, having a picnic, going for a hike, watching a movie, playing a computer game, fishing or hunting, photography, or reading a favorite book. Sometimes we engage in spontaneous activities, such as jumping in a swimming pool with our clothes on, spraying someone with a hose while washing the car, or playing a practical joke on a friend. At other times, we plan our fun like going to Disney World for a week, taking a month-long excursion through the Orient, or scuba diving along the Great Barrier Reef.

We can experience enjoyment doing things we normally don't associate with pleasure. For instance, folding clothes, doing dishes, pulling weeds, or cleaning the bathroom are tasks that score low on the "fun" scale for most people. However, we can make these tasks more enjoyable by considering the joy that these activities bring us. Pulling weeds, for example, will yield a beautiful flower bed or a bountiful garden even though it can be a tedious and often uncomfortable task.

Living a life of integrity, honor, and purpose does not mean that we have to live a life devoid of fun, joy, and happiness. What matters the most is results. Too many people think that work or other necessary tasks need to be laborious and painful. We don't have to live that way. God does not want us to be bitter and unhappy. Will we have a more positive impact on the world around us if we are bitter and unhappy or loving, happy, and joyful?

Let's take a look at one of nature's creatures that is a good example for having fun and experiencing enjoyment. Consider the otter; they play like a child at recess on the playground. When the snow piles deep, they will find a suitable hill and take turns sliding down the hill on their backs. Although otters don't smile, it almost appears that they do when they are enjoying themselves. Otters are very good hunters and take care of their young; however they mix a healthy amount of play into their lives. An example is the sea otters that live off the coast of California. They will swim on their backs and crack open mussels that they have pulled from the ocean floor below. When they finish eating, they frolic in the water like they are part fish.

The North American river otter is a cousin to the weasel, martin, skunk, badger, and mink. It weighs about fifteen to twenty-five pounds, has a long slender body (males can reach a length of four feet), and is covered with thick waterproof fur. The otter is at home in the water, although it spends much time on the land and is an amazingly good runner (they lope instead of run). They typically live ten years in the wild, but have been known to live up to twenty years in captivity.

The river otter's main diet consists of fish like catfish, suckers (carp and buffalo), sunfish, and bluegill. They also eat frogs, toads, turtles, crayfish, salamanders, mussels, muskrats, birds, rodents, and snakes. They have even been known to eat beaver. They mostly hunt at night; however they will hunt and eat any time of the day. Otters use their long sensitive whiskers to find prey in the murky river water and catch their prey using their mouth—other otter species use their hands (or front paws).

River otters can dive to a depth of fifty-five feet and can hold their breath for several minutes. They have special valves that keep water out of their noses and ears. Their long powerful tail, slender body, and webbed feet make them excellent swimmers. Using their whiskers to help them find their way, they can swim through brushy and tangled debris with great ease. Otters are graceful creatures and yet surprisingly quick and maneuverable on both land and in the water.

Otters sometimes hunt in packs, especially when they are hunting fish. They work together to push fish into a shallow alcove and then snatch them as they try to escape. At other times they are solitary and scrounge through the rocks and muddy river bottom looking for an unsuspecting catfish, turtle, or crayfish.

River otters are territorial and mark their terrain with a scent produced by glands on their back legs. Otter territories rarely overlap if they are of the same sex; however a male otter's territory will often overlap several female territories. Otters are usually tolerant of other otters, except during mating season when the males get aggressive towards each other.

Otters have a high metabolism and require frequent meals. It only takes a few hours for a meal to pass completely through their system. This high metabolism gives the otter seemingly boundless energy and keeps them warm in the water. A high energy level may be one of the reasons that they play so much.

Female otters will have two or three pups each year, although they can have as many as five. She nurses her pups for three or four months depending on availability of food and growth of the pups. They nest in secluded places like a hollow log, an abandoned beaver lodge, or a hole in the ground along a stream or lake. The pups will stay with their mother for a year until they are old enough to fend for themselves. The pups are natural swimmers; however the mother often has to coax them into the water the first time. They sometimes ride on the back of their mother. Sounds like fun!

What attracts most people to the otter is its carefree and playful attitude, although I'm sure a fish, turtle, or bird that gets in the otter's path may think otherwise. They seem to enjoy themselves year around. If otters were human, they would live in California on the beach and work in Silicon Valley (home of the high-pressure software business)—they work hard and play hard. They have been seen taking turns body surfing down a snow bank, sliding in mud, and frolicking in water—playing an otter's version of water polo. This playful spirit starts when they are old enough to open their eyes (two to three weeks after birth) and continues until they are old.

So how can we apply the otter's carefree spirit to our lives? The best way to answer this is to look at a bad example first. Let's look at the parable of the prodigal son:

> There was a man who had two sons. The younger one said to his father, "Father, give me my share of the estate." So he divided his property between them.
>
> Not long after that, the younger son got together all he had, set off for a distant country and there squandered his wealth in wild living. After he had spent everything, there was a severe famine in that whole country, and he began to be in need. So he went and hired himself out to a citizen of that country, who sent him to his fields to feed pigs. He longed to fill his stomach with the pods that the pigs were eating, but no one gave him anything.
>
> When he came to his senses, he said, "How many of my father's hired men have

food to spare, and here I am starving to death! I will set out and go back to my father and say to him: Father, I have sinned against heaven and against you. I am no longer worthy to be called your son; make me like one of your hired men." So he got up and went to his father.

But while he was still a long way off, his father saw him and was filled with compassion for him; he ran to his son, threw his arms around him and kissed him.

The son said to him, "Father, I have sinned against heaven and against you. I am no longer worthy to be called your son."

But the father said to his servants, "Quick! Bring the best robe and put it on him. Put a ring on his finger and sandals on his feet. Bring the fattened calf and kill it. Let's have a feast and celebrate. For this son of mine was dead and is alive again; he was lost and is found." So they began to celebrate.

Meanwhile, the older son was in the field. When he came near the house, he heard music and dancing. So he called one of the servants and asked him what was going on. "Your brother has come," he replied, "and your father has killed the fattened calf because he has him back safe and sound."

The older brother became angry and refused to go in. So his father went out and pleaded with him. But he answered his father, "Look! All these years I've been slaving for you and never disobeyed your orders. Yet you never gave me even a young goat so I could celebrate with my friends. But when this son of yours who has squandered your property with prostitutes comes home, you kill the fattened calf for him!"

"My son," the father said, "you are always with me, and everything I have is yours. But we had to celebrate and be glad, because this brother of yours was dead and is alive again; he was lost and is found."

—Luke 15:11-32

This younger son lived "wild" and spent his money foolishly on wine, women, and song. In today's world, that may be translated as getting drunk, having sex, taking drugs, and living without regard for self or others. In our modern society, many people would say this young man was just "having fun." But is this the kind of fun an otter would have? Is it the kind of fun that will bring long-lasting joy to your life?

Let's look at what happened to the young son: He spent all his money on reckless living and had to go to work for a pig farmer. Then a famine hit and he nearly starved to death. He was so hungry he wanted to eat the pig's food! This often happens to those who live recklessly. They get strung out on drugs, become an alcoholic, or contract a serious disease. This often leads to a life of crime (i.e., stealing to support their lifestyle). As a result, they may become unemployable except for the least desirable jobs. This is clearly not the kind of fun that builds character or brings lasting enjoyment to our lives.

Fortunately for the prodigal son, he realized that he was not living a joyful life and returned home to his father. He learned his lesson the hard way. How often do we have to experience the pain of doing things that don't honor us before we correct it?

Let's look at the prodigal son as he could have lived his life. He wanted to see the world around him and to see how people lived in another land; that's why he asked for his inheritance. He also wanted to enjoy himself as he traveled. How might he have approached this? He could still have gone to his father and asked for money to travel and even agreed to pay it back when he returned. Instead of wine, women, and song (alcohol, sex, and drugs), he could have enjoyed the beautiful scenery, the smells of the desert, the sounds of wild birds, and the exotic food from a local inn.

To keep him company, he could have asked a friend who shares his convictions to travel with him. The two could have laughed and sang songs while traveling. Camping in the open night air would have been exhilarating and telling stories by the campfire would have been comforting. When they returned, he and his friend would have stories to tell for years to come. In his later years, he could have recalled this adventure with a smile and would have been able to relive the joy again. He could have experienced a joy that didn't rob him of his future.

Let's look at the lessons of the otter:

- Otters have fun wherever they are—enjoy your life whether you are at work or play. We are not guaranteed tomorrow and yesterday is gone.

- Otters live responsible lives even while they have fun—do not make fun the center of your life. Happiness and joy are the results of living a balanced, responsible life.

- Otters are serious when the situation calls for it—it is not always appropriate to have fun. There is a time and place for enjoyment. An example where it wouldn't be appropriate is a funeral or wake (although there are some who do have fun).

- Otters enjoy fun that does not cause them harm—choose entertainment that does not cause you or others harm. Learn the lessons of the prodigal son.

- Otters encourage others to play—involve others in your enjoyment. You can bring joy to someone else's life and increase your joy in the process.

- Otters pass on their gift to their young—teach others a joyful way to live. You may save a life and a soul.

So how do we add enjoyment into our lives? First, be thankful that you are alive. Of all the possibilities, God chose you to be born and to be here on this third planet from the sun. What a living marvel you are! Your body contains trillions of cells all working together to create a living, breathing human being. You are unique!

Second, God loves you and knows how many hairs are on your head. Do you know how many hairs are on your head? If you are that important that your hairs are numbered, then what a great joy!

Third, we have all been given talents and we are here to serve a purpose. This alone brings me happiness. How about you? Even if you don't yet know what your talents are or what your purpose is, this should stir your soul. Think of it; you exist for a special purpose.

Fourth, pray for guidance and understanding. This step alone will lead you to living the kind of joy-filled life that may have escaped you to this point. As the best selling author and public speaker Mark Victor Hansen has said, "Prayer works."

Finally, look closely at your life. Are there ways to make your tasks joyful? If it is difficult to find something to be happy about rent a funny movie or go to a comedy show. Laughter has been shown to reduce stress, lower blood pressure, release endorphins (brain chemicals that make us feel good), and increase our immunity. Joy and laughter is healthy. Make it part of your daily diet.

To learn more about otters visit your local zoo or search on the internet for "river otter" and follow the links. If you are fortunate to live near a stream, lake, or river, then go otter watching. Learn from one of nature's most joyful creatures.

The otter is happy and playful, too,
Perhaps there is no day when an otter is blue.
Learn from the otter and add joy to your life,
Happiness will fill you and drive out the strife.

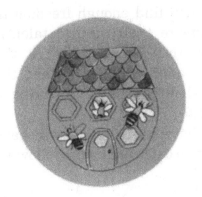

Chapter 5

Family Life of Honeybees

Children obey your parents in everything,
for this pleases the Lord.
Colossians 3:20

A family is defined as the basic unit in society traditionally consisting of two parents rearing their own or adopted children. However, today many families are headed by a single adult. This is not as God designed it from the beginning. For our purposes, we will look at a family as it was originally designed. The reason for this is that God's original design is the best approach to raising children and giving them the tools to lead a successful and purpose driven life. It's also the best design for happiness and fulfillment for everyone in the family.

The most important aspect of any family is that there is love for one another and that God is the center of their life. A father and mother cannot expect to set a good example to their children unless they love each other. This kind of love is patient, kind, honest, and unconditional. A deep abiding love can be a fountain of strength for everyone in the family. A small child will trust enough to take their first steps. A teenager will find enough freedom to spread their wings, explore their natural talents, and become the person they aspire to be. At the same time, this young adult will know that the family is a rock that they can swim to during a stormy period in their life.

The kind of love that a husband and wife have for one another can best be captured by the following passage:

"But at the beginning of creation God made them male and female. For this reason a man will leave his father and mother and be united to his wife, and the two will become one flesh. So they are no longer two, but one."
—Mark 10:6-8

The husband and wife are one. They are united in purpose to raise up godly children. These children will grow to have families of their own and they will use what they learned in their youth and pass it on to their children.

"Train up a child in the way he should go, even when he is old he will not depart from it."
—Proverbs 22:6

Children and young adults should have this same kind of love for their parents. While there may be times when they disagree with their parents and maybe even fight with them, they know that their parents love them and want the best for them. This is true regardless of age (i.e., whether eight, eighteen, or fifty-eight years old). This doesn't mean that parents are always right. They may be wrong and often are. However, the family should work out all conflicts in the spirit of love.

"Children, obey your parents in everything,
for this pleases the Lord."
—Colossians 3:20

"Fathers, do not embitter your children,
or they will become discouraged."
—Colossians 3:21

There are families that do not share this view. Some parents do not show their love, either because they do not know how or because they are incapable of caring for another human being. In those situations, it is best to seek outside help.

A great example of a close family working together for a common purpose is a hive of honeybees. All honeybees work together as a family unit to both protect and ensure the survival of the hive. During the peak honey season, the average worker bee will only live four to six weeks. They literally work themselves to death. Their entire being is subordinated to the health and welfare of the hive.

Before we get into the family life of the honeybee we need to provide some background. Honeybees are native to Europe, Asia, and the Middle East and were brought to North America by the early European settlers. Since then, they have become a critical link in pollinating orchards, vineyards, and other farm crops. Examples of plants that they pollinate are blueberries, blackberries, watermelon, apples, raspberries, strawberries, cherries, cranberries, clover, and many types of grasses. They supply us with honey, pollen, beeswax, and a substance called royal jelly (bees produces this from glands in their heads), which is eaten as a nutritional supplement. In addition, the venom from their stings is being harvested and used as possible treatment for some types of diseases and afflictions, such as arthritis.

Honeybees have been domesticated for thousands of years. Early hives consisted of a basket with a hole to allow access for the bees. Harvesting honey from these early hives often resulted in the destruction of the colony. Modern hives allow beekeepers to take honey from the hive without jeopardizing the colony or injuring the bees.

Inside the hive you will find one queen, anywhere from zero to over a thousand drones (male bees), depending on the time of year, and twenty thousand to fifty thousand workers. The life span of the queen is five years, the workers and the drones typically live four to six weeks in the summer. Over the winter a worker can live five or six months. Drones are kicked out of the hive in the fall and starve to death.

Fertilized eggs can become either a worker or a queen. Workers are fed royal jelly for the first three days of their life. Thereafter, they are fed honey and pollen. The queen is fed royal jelly her entire life. This difference in food determines whether an egg will be a worker or a queen. Queens are only produced when the hive queen dies or when the hive becomes too crowded and they swarm. When a hive swarms, most of the workers leave with the departing queen. The workers gorge themselves on honey and then fly off to find a new home leaving behind a small colony that will quickly grow large again.

Let's take a closer look at the individuals that make up the hive. The queen is the center of the hive and is constantly attended to by workers. The queen is longer than any other bee in the hive and is the only reproductive female. Her stinger is smooth and can be used repeatedly. She lacks all the special equipment for carrying pollen or making beeswax. Her primary job is to lay eggs. The queen can lay up to two thouand eggs a day, which is equivalent to her body weight. She lays fertilized eggs (workers) and unfertilized eggs (drones). The queen inspects each cell before laying an egg. If the cell is too small or deformed, she will pass it up and workers will immediately begin modifying the cell.

The workers, which make up most of the hive, are nonreproductive females. Although female like the queen, their stingers are barbed and can be used only once. If they do use their stinger, they will tear out their internal organs and die shortly afterward. A worker truly gives its life by defending the hive. In addition to the barbed stinger, they have specialized baskets on their legs for carrying pollen and glands on their abdomen that secrete wax for building the comb. They also have a special honey sac that is used to convert nectar into honey. Workers do all the work in the hive except lay eggs. Under certain conditions they can lay unfertilized eggs that turn into drones.

Drones are the other specialized bees in the group. They are male and their only task is to mate with a queen. In this task they have to outrace all their competition to catch the queen—she's the fastest flying bee in the hive. They don't have a stinger, can't produce honey or wax, and don't have any equipment to collect pollen. Because they are useless to the hive, they are all kicked out of the hive in the fall and they starve to death. This may sound cruel, however the bees have a tough time in the winter and they don't want to feed anyone who doesn't contribute to the group.

The honeybee starts its life as an egg at the bottom of a half inch deep hexagonal wax cell. Let's call this honeybee Daisy. She is a worker bee like all of her sisters. Daisy is fed and nursed by her older sisters from the day her mother laid an egg in the bottom of the cell until she emerges some twenty-one days later as a fully grown, but immature, bee. During this time Daisy is fed a diet of royal jelly (a substance secreted by glands in her sisters' heads), honey, and pollen.

After emerging from her cell, she begins working inside the hive as a cell cleaner. Her job is to clean out any waste and to polish the cell in preparation for a new sister. After Daisy finishes the cell, her mother inspects it and then lays an egg. Daisy moves on to another cell and repeats the whole process. It's like cleaning up a nursery room in preparation for a new baby.

A few days later Daisy graduates from cleaning cells and begins repairing them. Some cells get damaged when her sisters emerge from them.

She secretes flakes of wax from glands in her abdomen and then puts them into place with her mouth. As she gets better at this, she joins her other sisters in making new cells.

While Daisy is building new cells, she notices that some of her other sisters are doing different tasks. Lilly was born on the same day as Daisy; however she was given the assignment of feeding their little sisters still living in cells. Lilly also carries off the waste that their very young sisters produce. It's sort of like changing diapers and feeding a baby with a bottle. Lilly eventually gets assigned to feed and care for their mother (the queen).

One sister is responsible for removing water out of the honey. Another fans her wings continuously at the entrance of the hive to provide circulation and to keep the hive at a constant temperature. Some even take up guard duty checking all the sisters returning from the field. The guards are necessary because some of the neighboring hives send out bees to steal honey.

After three weeks, Daisy gets assigned to the field. She now gets to forage for nectar and pollen and for the first time in her life she leaves the safety of the hive. On her first trip, she finds a dandelion and her instinct leads her to drink in all the nectar she can hold. Almost without thinking about it, she collected enough pollen to fill her two pollen sacs on her back legs. Daisy was unaware that she had done a great service to the dandelion patch by carrying pollen from one flower and leaving it at another.

She did notice that there were thousands of flowers and she got excited and wanted to tell all her sisters about her find. When she arrived back at the hive, she immediately communicated her find by dancing a special bee dance. The dance tells her sisters which direction to fly, how far to fly, and how big the find is. As Daisy twists and shakes, her sisters watch her every move. After completing her dance, hundreds of her sisters fly off to the dandelion patch.

Daisy lives her remaining life (three weeks) foraging in the field with her sisters. Meanwhile, in the hive, a new generation of sisters are preparing to take her place. All the bees work together to secure a future for their family. And the bee goes on.

What can we learn from Daisy and the rest of her family? Your list may look something like this:

- Bees are devoted to the hive and to each other.
- Bees share their food with each other.
- Bees clean house.
- Bees change diapers and feed the babies.
- Bees use all their talents.
- Bees defend the family.
- Bees produce a surplus.
- Bees communicate.
- Bees fix and repair the house.
- Bees respect and honor their parents.
- Bees take responsibility.
- Bees work.
- Bees share their excitement with their family.
- Bees make the world around them better.
- Bees serve others.

- Bees live in a house full of sisters and there is no fighting.

Are there ways you can learn from Daisy? Here's a list of questions you can use to help you:

- Are you devoted to your family? How do you express your devotion? If you're not devoted, why not?
- Do you share with others in your family? Do they share with you?
- Do you help around the house? What could you do to help the family?
- Do you use all your talents? Are there things you can do that you don't currently do?
- Do you encourage others in your family?

ഇൗ

Honeybee busy from the day you were born,
Always dedicated to your family and never forlorn.
You set an example for me to pursue,
I will love my family in everything I do.

Chapter 6

Trees Seek Out the Light

This is the message we have heard from him and declare to you: God is light; in him there is no darkness at all. If we claim to have fellowship with him yet walk in the darkness, we lie and do not live by the truth. But if we walk in the light, as he is in the light, we have fellowship with one another, and the blood of Jesus, his son, purifies us from all sin.
1 John 1:5-7

Our lives are to be spent living in pursuit of truth and knowledge. Man's quest for truth and meaning has dominated the thoughts of philosophers, sages, gurus, and the wise for thousands of years.

What is truth? Many argue about the definition of truth or what true enlightenment really means. Before we answer that question, let's define the meaning of the word truth. Webster's dictionary defines truth as the body of real things, events, and facts or sincerity in action, character, and utterance. Knowledge is defined as the fact or condition of knowing something with familiarity gained through experience, association, or acquaintance with or understanding of a science, art, or technique. What a mouthful. Basically, truth and knowledge is knowing something is fact without a doubt. For example, if you burned your finger on a hot stove, there is no doubt that your finger hurts. The statement, "My finger hurts," is true. You have knowledge that the stove is hot because you gained it through experience (burning your finger).

Truth is important in everything we do. Our court system works on the presumption that both sides get to tell their story and the judge and jury sift through this testimony to find the truth. We depend on truth to buy a milk shake. If the milk shake costs $1.50 and we give the cashier $2.00, we know we are entitled to 50 cents in change. We will always get back 50 cents in that situation because 50 cents plus $1.50 always equals $2.00. This is what is called absolute truth. It's true in New York, Chicago, Los Angeles, and the moon (if you could buy a $1.50 milk shake on the moon).

The fact that you know $1.50 plus 50 cents equals $2.00 is called knowledge. Knowledge is important because we can use it to make good decisions and to avoid mistakes. A surgeon, through years of education, gains knowledge of the human body and the tools necessary to practice medicine. For example, a brain surgeon must understand the human brain very well, because one misstep or wrong cut could paralyze the patient or worse, kill them.

Where do we find the fountain of truth for how we are supposed to live our lives? What is right and what is wrong? Once we find it, how do we grow strong in truth and knowledge? How do we stay the course? Let's consider the following passage:

"For God, who said, 'Let light shine out of darkness,' made his light shine in our hearts to give us the light of the knowledge of the glory of God in the face of Christ."
—2 Corinthians 4:6

Light (truth and knowledge) comes from God. It is the source of energy for living a good and prosperous life. If we are shaded from the light, we will die like a plant would die without the sun. A good example of the power of light can be found in nature. Plants need light to live and grow. Perhaps the most majestic and awe inspiring living thing in the plant kingdom is the tree. The trees in the forest live off the light from the sun. Without it, they would die. Let's take a closer look at trees.

Trees come in all shapes and sizes and are some of the largest organisms in the world. Some live very long lives, over four thousand years, like the sequoia; others live relatively short lives like the common willow. Most trees live out their entire lives in one location, however some species of trees can move to better locations such as aspens. Aspen trees grow in clumps off of a common root system and can migrate to a more favorable location by growing shoots in the desired direction.

All trees fight for survival and employ various strategies to ensure their future as well as that of their seeds. For example, walnut trees use a form of chemical warfare to kill trees of another species. The walnut produces a poison through its roots which can inhibit the growth of other trees. The hard maple, commonly called the sugar maple, has very dense foliage and shades out almost all plants except for the most shade tolerant, such as some species of fern, ginseng, moss, et cetera.

Some species of trees grow very slowly, such as the bristlecone pine of the southwestern United States; others grow very quickly, like the poplar, which is often used as a windbreak in the prairie states where winds can blow for days at a time. The growth rate of trees depends on the environmental factors of the area where they are growing and on the genetics of the species. For example, the cottonwood trees that grow on the shores of the Mississippi River can reach heights over one hundred feet and tower over other species of trees that share this shoreline habitat. These cottonwoods grow straight and can attain diameters of six feet or greater. Further west, in the plains that stand in the shadows of the Rocky Mountains, these same cottonwoods are often gnarled, crooked, and seldom grow taller than fifty or sixty feet. The soil conditions and the lack of water are primary causes for the condition of these western cottonwoods. However, there is another factor that affects the growth of these trees: sunlight.

Light is important to all plant life. Plants use a process called photosynthesis to generate the food (sugars) they need to grow. Photosynthesis uses chlorophyll (the green pigment) to manufacture sugars such as glucose, sucrose, et cetera. This green color is caused by the chlorophyll reflecting the green light from the sun. Plants use water and carbon dioxide in conjunction with light to produce their food and they give off oxygen, which we need to live. Plants and animals form a symbiotic relationship, which means they each produce something that the other needs to survive.

Along the banks of the Mississippi River, many trees compete for the nutrients in the soil, water, and sunlight. The competition for sunlight is fierce. Some trees grow more quickly than others around them. They are soon much taller than their neighbors and are able to soak up the sun's rays unobstructed. They are able to grow tall and straight as a result. Other trees grow in odd directions even leaning out over the river to get their share of the sun. Some can't compete by growing taller, so they soak up the sunlight filtering through the other trees. A good example of this is the dogwood tree.

The dogwood is used to not having full sunlight and compensates for this by having leaves that are more sensitive to light. They are able to grow even though other trees tower over them in the forest. The dogwood has such a thick canopy that no other trees can live under them in the forest. They grab all the light they can get!

Another interesting example is the Missouri (hardy) pecan tree. This tree is similar to its southern cousin; however the pecans are smaller and taste sweeter. The pecan tree sends out limbs in all directions growing in odd shapes and bushing out to gather the sunlight. If the pecan doesn't have any other trees around it, it will grow to look similar to a giant ball setting on a tree trunk. In other words, it gathers every bit of light available to it.

Trees offer a great example to us. They take whatever path is available to them to bask in the warm life-giving rays of the sun. If they can't or don't get sunlight, they will die. In fact trees die quickly without sunlight. They will only live a few short days in this condition and will soon whither away.

We are like trees. We need to bask in the light from the Master or we too will die. Sure our bodies may live on until we are old; however our souls are dead without the life-giving light of God. Just as the leaves fall off the tree when it is robbed of sunlight, so too will our leaves fall if we don't drink up our daily portion of the life-giving light. We can see the dead leaves of those who don't seek truth and knowledge. They live miserable lives seeking truth in money, drugs, alcohol, or some other substitute or artificial light. Their outsides seem fine; however they are hollowed out like a dying oak tree that looks strong on the outside, but is dead on the inside. Just as the oak falls over in a big storm, so, too, does this person fall when the storms of life hit them. They have not been prepared on the inside to handle problems, so they collapse.

So how do we find the light and then follow it? First, light comes from God. We find the path to a good life spelled out in the Bible. The Old Testament is filled with stories, proverbs, and examples on how to live, eat, wash dishes, and grow spiritually. Incidentally, the Israelites were to dry their dishes in the sun. We know today that drying dishes in the sun kills germs. Of course they didn't know about germs. Their neighbors, the Egyptians, who were considered educated, believed that rubbing cat feces into a wound would help it to heal! We now know this would introduce germs. It's a wonder that the Egyptians survived.

The New Testament is filled with guidance that can be summed up as follows:

- Love your God with all your heart, soul, and mind.

- Love your neighbor as yourself.

Of course, it includes parables, stories, and examples on living a godly life.

Second, pray for guidance and understanding. The Master said in the book of Luke:

"So I say to you: Ask and it will be given to you; seek and you will find; knock and the door will be opened to you."
—Luke 11:9

This is one of the most powerful tools we have available to us. It is like the leaves filled with chlorophyll that are able to convert sunlight into energy. We, through prayer, can turn God's light into a good life and energy for our souls.

Third, gather other light-seeking people around you. Like the trees that grow straight and tall when competing for sunlight, we also grow straight and tall on the inside when we are striving for the light. Start from where you are. If you live in an environment that is shading the light, then grow in the direction where you can get more light. An example would be if you have friends who push you away from godly truth or who are bad examples, then avoid their company. Do not let other trees shade out your light. Grow past them! Your love and calm spirit may change them into light seeking trees.

Finally, make this a life-long quest. We can never be over exposed to the light. Just as trees continue to add growth rings each year and become extremely strong, so can we if we bask in the light. We must always grow and learn, just like a tree. When a tree quits growing, it dies. If we quit growing and learning, we die on the inside.

If you live next to a tract of woods or park, take a walk through the woods and observe the trees. What do you see? How are they growing? Look for dogwoods or other shade-tolerant trees that inhabit the forest floor. Are they getting by or are they thriving? Are there any dead or dying trees? Do you see any that are losing leaves?

After the walk, sit down and write out three things that you could change that would allow you to get more light into your life. Ask someone to help you live up to these changes. Even better, ask someone to participate with you. Do it together. After you do it awhile, you should start to see the strong growth rings in your life.

❧

Trees grow strong living in the light,
Growing from little saplings to great height.
We can learn from their example and grow, too,
Seeking the life-giving light in everything we do.

Chapter 7

Dogs and Loyalty

But the lord is faithful, and he will
strengthen and protect you from the evil one.
2 Thessalonians 3:3

Loyalty is often described as faithfulness, relia-
bility, dependability, fidelity, commitment, alle-
giance, duty, and dedication. Loyalty is integrity to
commitment. It's being honest with yourself with
respect to your commitments. It is essential to be
loyal to your commitments. Imagine for a moment
that your best friend, a member of your family, or
someone else that you trust very much betrayed you.
Suppose that you could not trust anyone. What
would that feel like? What kind of life would we have
if we couldn't trust others? We depend on others and
we must trust others. Loyalty is essential in a
marriage. It is essential in a friendship. It is essential in our service to God. God is loyal to us. We need
only be loyal to Him.

"Jesus replied: 'Love the Lord your God with all
your heart and with all your soul and with all your
mind. This is the first and greatest commandment.'"
—Matthew 22:37-38

Is there room in the above verse for loving God with most of your heart? Or all of your heart and some of your mind? How about all of your heart and all of your soul, but part of your mind? All of these situations are not loyal to God. God asks for everything. That is loyalty. In return you get all of God. What a great relationship.

This dedication is essential in all relationships where loyalty is required. But first, let's talk about some relationships where loyalty is good, but not essential. Whether you buy your groceries from the same store or multiple stores is irrelevant to how you live your life. It may be relevant to the grocer, but it is not essential that you be loyal to a particular merchant. Sometimes it can matter. I purchase and service my car at the same auto dealer because they treat me well. I'm loyal to them to a point. If they started mistreating me, I would probably take my business elsewhere.

You can choose to be loyal to whoever or whatever you choose. However, every choice has consequences—some good and some not so good. For example, you can choose to be loyal to money; however this is not what God asks of us. So, by default, you can't be loyal to God if you put anything else ahead of Him. This is not to say that the pursuit of money is bad, it is not. God wants us to have healthy and abundant lives. I, personally, have some very large money goals; however these goals have not been put ahead of God—they, include God financially.

The first rule is to be careful of giving your loyalty to other people or things. We must be careful to choose friends worthy of our loyalty. Our friends should be people who share similar values with us. You would not want to be loyal to someone who is a car thief. This so-called friend would eventually involve us in their illegal activity. Once we have a friend worthy of us, then we should be loyal to them.

> *"A true friend is always loyal,*
> *and a brother is born to help in time of need."*
> —Proverbs 17:17

The second rule is that loyalty is never ending. God asks for our total loyalty. There is no end to this loyalty. We don't choose to be loyal to God in the good times and then turn our backs on Him when things go sour. God asks for total loyalty. Often when things are bad, God has not abandoned us, but rather is carrying us through.

> *"Never tire of loyalty and kindness. Hold these virtues*
> *tightly. Write them deep within your heart."*
> —Proverbs 3:3-4

The third rule (or corollary) is that loyalty brings happiness and peace of mind. If you get married and you worry that your spouse is not true (loyal) to you, how much happiness or peace of mind will you have? Not much. On the other hand, a truly loyal friend brings trust, sharing, compassion, integrity, honor, and love. These are qualities that make our lives meaningful and joyful. Consider the following passage:

After David had finished talking with Saul, Jonathan became one in spirit with David, and he loved him as himself. From that day Saul kept David with him and did not let him return to his father's house. And Jonathan made a covenant with David because he loved him as himself. Jonathan took off the robe he was wearing and gave it to David, along with his tunic, and even his sword, his bow and his belt.

—1 Samuel 18:1-4

In nature, there is one animal that comes to mind when the word loyalty is used—the dog. Dogs are probably the most loyal animals on earth. I know that some may argue that a horse can be loyal too (I've owned a very loyal Tennessee walking horse). I would agree that there are other loyal animals; however the dog is the most universally loyal pet and companion that man has ever domesticated. The dog has protected cities, assisted the blind, fought battles, hunted killers, protected families and property, and has given its life for its companions.

Stories of dogs jumping off cliffs, fighting bears and wolves, waiting for a dead master, and saving people from danger are common place. Dogs do seem to have a sixth sense that gives them the ability to know when things are not right. They have become part of our families and will often guard them ferociously.

When I was about ten years old, I had a beagle named Sports. We hunted rabbits together and he would actually point for a covey of quail—a trait normally associated with bird dogs. When we went out for the day, I would bring him a sandwich to eat as well. I learned to feed him a few bites at a time; otherwise he would eat his in one or two bites and then look longingly at me for the rest of mine. I would talk to him for hours and he would cock his head as though he understood every word. As a result of this close relationship, he would not allow anyone to harm me. Once a bully showed up in our front yard and proceeded to wrestle me to the ground. Sports heard my yelling and attacked the bully. The bully ran and we both chased him up the road. I loved that dog.

Dogs have been domesticated for thousands of years and there are as many different breeds of dogs as there are owners (or at least it seems like it). There are small lap dogs like the teacup poodle and large dogs like the Great Dane and malamute. Each breed was originally bred for some particular purpose. The poodle was bred in France as a hunting dog. The malamute was bred to withstand the cold and pull sleds in the snow. Probably one of the most universal breeds is the German shepherd. Originally bred in Germany as a work dog, they have been used to guide the blind, search out drugs or explosives, and as protection. All these dogs are very loyal and dependable.

Movies and TV shows have been made to show the loyalty of dogs. Some examples include *Old Yeller, Lassie,* and *Rin Tin Tin.* Dogs are very smart and can be trained to do all sorts of tasks. One of the more amazing feats are dogs that have been trained to look for and find cancer.

Probably the best testimony for importance of the dog as man's best friend comes from a court case in Missouri:

In Warrensburg, Missouri, in 1870, a court case (Burden vs. Hornsby) was held involving a man who killed his neighbor's dog for chasing sheep. As the story goes, Charles Burden had a hunting dog named Old Drum. His neighbor and brother-in-law, Leonidas Hornsby, threatened to kill any dog that killed his sheep. Although Hornsby never saw Old Drum kill any sheep, he suspected that he had in the past. One evening, Hornsby found a dog prowling in his yard and he shot it. It was Old Drum. Charles Burden immediately sued Hornsby for damages.

Charles enlisted the services of George Graham Vest, later to become Senator, as his attorney. At one point in the trial Vest made the following plea to the jury:

"The best friend a man has in this world may turn against him and become his enemy. His son or daughter that he has reared with loving care may prove ungrateful. Those who are nearest and dearest to us, those whom we trust with our happiness and our good name, may become traitors to their faith. The money that a man has, he may lose. It flies away from him, perhaps when he needs it the most. A man's reputation may be sacrificed in a moment of ill-considered action. The people who are prone to fall on their knees to do us honor when success is with us may be the first to throw the stone of malice when failure settles its cloud upon our heads. The one absolutely unselfish friend that a man can have in this selfish world, the one that never deserts him and the one that never proves ungrateful or treacherous is his dog.

"Gentleman of the Jury, a man's dog stands by him in prosperity and in poverty, in health and in sickness. He will sleep on the cold ground, where the wintry winds blow and the snow drives fiercely, if only he may be near his master's side. He will kiss the hand that has no food to offer, he will lick the wounds and sores that encounter the roughness of the world. He guards the sleep of his pauper master as if he were a prince. When all other friends desert, he remains. When riches take wings and reputation falls to pieces, he is as constant in his love as the sun in its journey through the heavens.

"If fortune drives the master forth an outcast in the world, friendless and homeless, the faithful dog asks no higher privilege than that of accompanying him to guard against danger, to fight against his enemies. When the last scene of all comes, and death takes the master in its embrace and his body is laid away in the cold ground, no matter if all other friends pursue their way, there by his graveside will the noble dog be found, his head between his paws, his eyes sad but open in alert watchfulness, faithful and true even to death."

The jury went on to award Charles Burden damages. The case was retried in the Missouri State Supreme court and Burden won again. In 1958, a statue was erected in Old Drum's honor in the town of Warrensburg.

What a beautiful story. What if we were able to show our friends, family, and God this kind of loyalty, how would it affect our lives? Do you have any relationships where you have not honored the other person with your loyalty? If someone accuses your friend of something while they're not present, do you defend them?

If you have a dog as a pet, watch it and observe their behavior. What happens when you come home? Does your dog greet you? We have several dogs (most live outside) that become very excited when I come home from work. They become so excited that I sometimes wonder whether they are going to shake themselves to pieces. What love and devotion. Do we have that kind of devotion for God?

Examine all your relationships. Are you loyal and devoted to them? Are these relationships worthy of your loyalty? Are they devoted to you? Use the humble dog as one of the best examples of loyalty that nature provides.

〰️
The dog is loyal and loving too,
Willing to follow and die for you.
God has done the same when He was man,
So be loyal like the dog if you can.

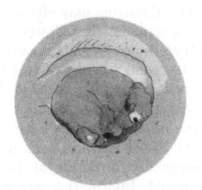

Chapter 8

Bears Need Rest

My soul finds rest in God alone;
my salvation comes from him.
Psalm 62:1

We need rest in order to function properly in the world. Our bodies must constantly build and repair damage done during our waking hours. Even God rested on the seventh day of creation. This was not because God was tired (how could God get tired?), but because He set an example for us to follow. In the Old Testament, Jewish law required that they rest on the Sabbath day (seventh day of the week). They were forbidden to cook, clean, harvest, and any other tasks that required them to walk very far from their home. These laws were so serious that violation was punishable by death.

In today's society, we have all but discarded the need for rest. Most major stores stay open twenty-four hours a day and seven days a week. Many work six and seven days a week and brag that they haven't taken a vacation in many years. Children go to school, play sports after hours, and do homework until late in the evening. On the weekends, everyone loads into vans and spends their days at soccer tournaments, wrestling play-offs, and band competitions. This is occasionally followed by event dinners and special occasions. What time does the average person have to spend actually resting?

Rest has been seen as a sign of weakness in our current culture. Amazingly, a few decades ago this was not the case. One need only watch a rerun of the *Andy Griffith Show* to see the laid back life that we used to lead (especially on Sundays). Our world is definitely fast paced. Information can be sent at the speed of light across microwave towers, satellites, or telephone wires. This information is usually acted on quickly—to postpone the response could cause a loss of opportunity or money or both. As a result, we have become a culture of information junkies that don't stray too far away from our computers. All this activity doesn't allow adequate rest. The result? Resting and avoiding the computer or participation in weekend events is perceived to be socially unacceptable. How can we succeed if we're not involved in every opportunity available to us?

We can't turn back the clock and we can't stop the flow of information. So how can we lead a life that includes adequate rest and relaxation in our modern, fast-paced world? Before we answer that question, let's look at nature for an example.

There are several examples we can use; however I think the bear best fits us. The bear rests. It doesn't actually hibernate (more about this later).

Bears live in North and South America, Europe, and Asia. They can be found in the coldest of climates (polar bear) as well as the warmest (sun bear). There are eight different species of bear: brown bear, giant panda, sun bear, spectacled bear, American Black bear, polar bear, Asiatic Black bear, and sloth bear. They range in size from the relatively small sun bear at 100 to 140 pounds to the polar bear that weighs nearly a ton.

Some bears have a very limited diet like the giant panda, which exclusively eats bamboo, and the polar bear, that eats primarily seals. Other bears have a varied diet that includes fruits, berries, nuts, insects, honey, rodents, fish, and virtually anything else that is edible. In the national parks throughout the United States visitors are warned to keep all food products locked up. Bears love sweets and will not pass up a good meal of marshmallows and hot dogs.

Bears have bulky bodies, very short tails, and large heads. Bears have small eyes and see in color, much the same as we do. Their best senses are hearing and smell. One of the reasons people get attacked is that they sneak through the woods and startle the bear. The first instinct of the bear is to retreat unless it feels cornered or has young cubs nearby. Bears can smell odors from more than a mile away. They have paws with claws that are not retractable like a lion or tiger and the males are larger than the females. Sometimes the male can be twice as large as the female.

Bears are solitary except for a mother and her cubs. Exceptions are when there is an abundance of food like a salmon run or when a huge patch of berries ripen. Not much is known about how bears communicate with one another. They use urine to mark territories and are furiously territorial to bears of the same sex.

Bears eat heartily when food is available and store fat for the winter. Tropical bears don't store fat for the winter since their food sources are available year around. When winter comes and food is no longer available, the bear goes into its den and sleeps.

Bears are not true hibernators like skunks and bats. Animals like bats and skunks hibernate and fall into a very deep sleep. Their body temperature falls close to freezing (just above thirty-two degrees Fahrenheit). Bears do not hibernate. When their food sources are no longer available in the winter, they will sneak off to a cave or hollow tree and go to sleep. Their body temperature will fall five to nine degrees Fahrenheit. Pregnant females will have their cubs in their cave and nurse them during this period. That is why a bear must put on so much fat.

During this resting phase, a bear's body has a chance to repair itself and recuperate from a long summer of feeding, fighting, and chasing prey. Some bears sleep through the entire winter, while others get up occasionally and roam. During these sleeping periods the bear does not defecate, urinate, eat, or drink. In addition, they have a safety mechanism to keep their temperatures from falling too low.

Man has been fascinated with bears since the time he lived in caves. Paintings of bears can be found throughout the world where bears live. Today, many people flock to parks and zoos to see bears and they are among the most popular attractions. I'm not any different. When we travel to the mountains we are always on the lookout for bears.

We can learn from this brawny beast. Rest is important to the bear especially in the winter when food is scarce. Without the ability of the bear to be able to slow its metabolism, many would starve to death before springtime. Without proper rest the bear could die. We are no different. We can't go long without sleep without serious side effects. Experiments have been conducted where people have volunteered to be sleep deprived for extended periods of time. In one particular instance, a radio DJ stayed awake for over a hundred hours. He stayed on the air and talked about his ordeal. Over time his thoughts and actions became bizarre. He had difficulty thinking and began to see imaginary images. Our bodies were not meant to go without rest.

Several years ago, my wife, Tammy, was pregnant with our oldest daughter. We had sold our house and moved in with my parents while we readied our house on our farm. In order to get our home ready in time for the baby, I would come home from work and then work on the house until late at night. I was losing sleep; however I thought I could manage it.

One evening, while we were attending Lamaze class at our local hospital, I passed out and slid out of my chair onto the floor. They rushed me to the emergency room and examined me from head to toe, literally. Finally the doctor gave me strict orders to go home and rest. The verdict? I was physically exhausted! He told me that the body will shut itself down when it gets in that condition. I should have paid more attention to my mother (and God's example).

From the beginning God set an example for us. He rested on the seventh day. Later Moses delivered the Ten Commandments and one of them said:

"Remember the Sabbath day by keeping it holy."
—Exodus 20:8

There is a physical lesson in this commandment. The word Sabbath means rest or an intermission. By resting we can devote our attention to God without distractions. It's our time to rest our minds and bodies and drink of the joys that God has bestowed on us the previous six days. Specifically in Exodus, God says:

"Six days you shall labor, but on the seventh day
you shall rest; even during the plowing season
and harvest you must rest."
—Exodus 34:21

Studies have shown that young adults who stayed up all night to prepare for a class or other task, showed little improvement for their efforts. What's worse is that sleeping for the next two nights had little effect as well. Losing sleep is detrimental. In college in the last twelve days of my senior year before graduating, I stayed up two nights without sleeping and only got three or four hours of sleep on the remaining nights. All of this was to prepare for finals. I did okay, but others who didn't pull an all nighter did better. After I graduated I went home and slept for seventeen hours straight!

Incidentally, when I get tired and miss too much sleep I notice that I startle easily. On a previous job, I use to have to work for extended periods of time that would sometimes last for twenty-four hours. When I drove home from work after these marathons, I would be jumpy and actually swerve to miss a butterfly. This is not as God had planned. We were not designed to push our bodies to total exhaustion.

There are serious health risks associated with lack of sleep. Studies have shown a marked increase in heart disease and diabetes in people who chronically miss too much sleep. Our insulin levels rise with a lack of sleep and this can lead to obesity. If you participate in physical activities like baseball or soccer, your performance will be directly linked to how rested you are. Many injuries result from not getting enough rest. You either overwork your muscles or cause yourself injury through poor judgment resulting from fatigue.

So how much rest is enough? A child needs as much as twelve or more hours of sleep. A young adult needs eight to nine hours a night. An adult needs approximately eight hours of sleep. Rest should be regular—like going to bed at the same time each night. If you have trouble sleeping because of worry, fold your hands in prayer and seek to lighten your heart. It's amazing what prayer can accomplish. The next time you think you can skip your rest with no ill effects, think of the brawny bear. Would the bear skip its rest?

Back to our original question: "How can we lead a life that includes adequate rest and relaxation in our modern fast-paced world?"

First, eliminate the unnecessary from your life. What in your life can you eliminate that will not adversely affect you or your family? For me, I eliminate watching excessive TV. I don't watch the news or any regular TV shows. I like old movies and occasionally watch learning programs offered on stations like the Discovery channel and the History channel.

Second, delegate when you can. Rather than mowing your yard, hire the boy up the street to do it. I hire my own children to do tasks like yard work, washing my car, cleaning the garage, and editing my book.

Third, follow the 80/20 rule; sometimes referred to as Pareto's Principle after the Italian mathematician, Vilfredo Pareto. According to this rule, 20 percent of things we do yield 80 percent of the results.

Fourth, plan for down time. I personally reserve Sunday afternoon for family time. My wife and I usually rest for a few hours. We talk and sometimes sleep. This rest period energizes me for the coming week.

Finally, prayer and meditation are good vehicles for rest and calming the mind. I usually relax, close my eyes, and visualize a scene from nature.

ॐ

Dear bear as you slumber this stormy night
Do you have your worries?
Is your mind filled with fright?
As I look at you so peaceful in your den
I think of God and the rest He has created for men.

Chapter 9

Spiders and Creativity

So God created man in his own image,
in the image of God he created him.
Genesis 1:27

Create is defined by Webster's New Collegiate Dictionary as to bring into existence or to produce by imaginative skill. The act of creation is a God-given talent. Nature is full of examples of things that create. As we will learn in Chapter 12, glaciers create great canyons, landscapes, and beauty. Birds build elaborate nests and bees build efficient and strong hexagonal structures that they use to store honey and rear their young. In fact, the honeycomb structure is so strong that we use the design in making aircraft. Yet, perhaps there is no more wonderful creation than the spider's web. The web is woven from material so complex and strong that we have not been able to duplicate it with the same efficiency. It is a beautiful creation. A single strand of web is pound for pound stronger than steel and yet delicate as a bubble floating on a summer breeze.

Before we get into the beauty and wonder of the spider's web, let's learn about the creature that has been immortalized in fable, rhyme, movie, and song.

There are nearly forty thousand different kinds of spiders in the world. Of these, some thirty-four thousand have been named. These spiders range in size from the tiny armored spider, which is the size of the head of a pin, up to the bird eating spider of the Brazilian rain forest, which can reach the size of a large dinner plate.

Spiders belong to a family of animals called arachnids and are related to scorpions, ticks, harvestmen (granddaddy longlegs), and mites. These animals have a head, abdomen, eight legs, fangs, and don't fly. Insects, on the other hand, have a head, thorax, and an abdomen; they have six legs and some of them fly. Spiders live on six of the seven continents and it has been estimated that they consume several tons of insects every year per acre of land. Without spiders, our world would be quickly overrun by six-legged creatures.

Spider silk has been used for all kinds of things. Soldiers during the Vietnam War used spider silk to staunch a bleeding wound. As recently as the 1940s, gun sights were made from spider silk. Several attempts have been made to use the silk for making clothing; however it takes so many spiders that it is impractical. In addition, spiders will eat each other if kept in close quarters. Silk worms are better suited for producing silk.

Many people are scared of spiders and recoil at the thought of touching one. Most of this fear comes from the mistaken belief that all spiders are poisonous, which is not true. Very few spiders are poisonous to man. In North America, there are only a couple of dangerous spiders; namely the black widow and the brown recluse (also known as the fatal fiddler because of the hour glass symbol on its back). The brown recluse is rarely fatal; however it can leave a nasty scar caused by its bite. The black widow can be fatal and has a very painful bite. Both of these spiders inhabit dark cool places like basements and crawl spaces under a house or old shed. Knowing where they live can help you avoid coming in contact with either of these arachnids.

Spiders are shy and territorial creatures and avoid humans when possible. The best places to look for spiders are in a garden, woods, or an orchard. A community park is a good location to find a variety of spiders. They are located where they can either ambush an unsuspecting insect as it wanders into its territory or trap it in an elaborate web made from spider silk. They will eat anything that they can overpower, including each other. The black widow female will often eat the male after mating. The male black widow is much smaller than the female and is often attacked and eaten while trying to mate with the larger female. When larger animals approach a spider, they will race for their burrow, which can be a hole in the ground or an old leaf.

Spiders are very creative in how they catch and kill their prey. Some ambush their prey by laying in wait such as the trap-door spider of Australia or the common wolf spider. The trap-door spider finds a small hole and builds a trap door over the entrance that matches the surroundings. It then waits inside for an unsuspecting insect such as a cricket to come too close. Once in range the spider bolts from its hole and injects the victim with venom. The venom consists of an agent that attacks the nervous system and digestive juices. It then drags the prey back into its lair where it consumes the contents once it liquefies.

Spiders create beautiful webs to catch their prey. There are several types of webs as follows:

- Orb web—which is the normal shape depicted in most drawings. It's circular and somewhat symmetrical.

- Triangle web—shaped like a triangle.

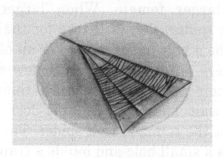

- Tangle web—looks messy. Typical shape used by the black widow.

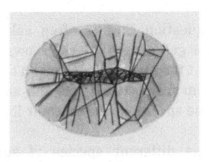

- Sheet web—mostly found in the woods.

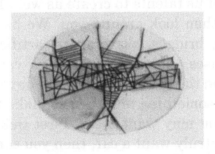

Spiders can build elaborate webs overnight. Many times I have taken a broom and removed webs that were built in the doorway, only to have them reappear the next morning. Once the web is complete the spider will hide and keep one of its legs fixed to a leader line. This leader line lets the spider know when something is trapped in its web. You can witness for yourself. Take a toothpick or straw and find a fresh spider web in the garden, woods, or park. Gently use the toothpick or straw to mimic a fly caught in a web. Usually the spider will appear from its hiding place and run towards the source of movement.

One question that is often asked is: "Why don't spiders get caught in their own web?" The answer is that they have special oil on their feet that prevents them from sticking to the surface of the web. They use special hooks on their legs to hold on to the web.

Just as different species of spiders make different kinds of webs, we have different creative talents. God created all things and we were created in the likeness of God. Many do not realize that God gave each of us talents to create as well. If you don't believe it, then look around you. We have created, cars, ships, bridges, skyscrapers, artificial hearts, contact lenses, poetry, music, art, relationships, families, and the list could go on. We have the ability to imagine something and then to make it real. For instance, you may want a car. First this is only an idea. If you truly want a car, then you can make the idea real by finding a means to pay for it and then purchase it. It works like this:

Idea > Action > Creation

This works for everything in your life. If you want to become a dentist, then you must train to become one. Once you have completed the proper schooling and passed the state exams, you can hang up your shingle and announce to the world that you are a dentist. If you want a better relationship with someone, the same rule applies. Whatever you conceive and believe, you can achieve.

Jesus told His disciples when they lacked enough faith, the following:

". . . I tell you the truth, if you have faith as small as a mustard seed, you can say to this mountain, 'Move from here to there' and it will move. Nothing will be impossible for you."
—Matthew 17:20-21

God does not limit us. We limit ourselves. We have talents to use in His service to help create a better world around us. But sadly, many people live their lives without ever exercising their talents and using them to create a better life. You don't have to create a skyscraper or write an opera to be creative. Maybe your talent is to encourage others to be all that God intended them to be. Or maybe your talent is to care for others when they are suffering. By exercising this talent you create a loving environment.

Working with others magnifies our creativity. Let's say you were given an assignment to raise $1000 for a school function. You could do it by yourself; however the task may take longer. Also, the number of ideas would be limited to your thoughts. For instance, you may think of using a bake sale or raffle to get the necessary funding. While these ideas are good, you may not think of other ways that could be easier or more valuable. Let's add a few more people to your team. You decide to brainstorm (a method for getting ideas on the table without judgment) and one of your teammates informs you that the local bank is looking to donate $500 for a charitable cause. You check into it and they agree to give the money to the school. Now you only have to raise $500 instead of $1000. This approach works for everything in your life. Remember that one of the most important team members is God.

The next time you're in the backyard or neighborhood park, take a closer look at the creative spider. Note how the webs look. See if you can identify the type of web and spider. How can you apply the creativity of the spider to your life? If someone knocks down your web (creation), build it back overnight like the spider. The spider will create a new web no matter how many times it gets knocked down. The web ensures its survival. We were put here to create better lives for others and just as the web ensures the future of the spider, so too, does creativity ensure our own survival.

<hr>

❧

Dear spider with too many legs and too many eyes,
You build your web to catch unsuspecting flies.
In your quest to catch and eat a meal,
You inspire me to create and my inaction to seal.

Chapter 10

Flowers Are Charitable

Remember this: Whoever sows sparingly will also reap sparingly, and whoever sows generously will also reap generously.
2 Corinthians 9:6

Charity is a beautiful word which means love and kindness and often refers to a gift freely given to someone in need. Probably the best definition comes from the book of John:

"For God so loved the world that he gave his one and only Son, that whoever believes in him shall not perish but have eternal life."
—John 3:16

What does the word charity bring to mind? Love? Giving freely to others? Being of service? Charity can be all of these and more.

Charity is like the Sea of Galilee. The sea is richly rewarded with a continual supply of water at the north end. The water provides sustenance for a great variety of life. Many types of fishes and birds live in its waters. The sea does not hoard its water, though. Out of the south of the sea flows water to match the water entering from the north.

The water flows freely from the Sea of Galilee into another body of water. The smaller sea is dead and lifeless. No fish or birds thrive in its waters. The sea is so filled with salt that you can almost lay on top of it. Many people from all over the world come to this sea to bathe and swim because of its heavy salt content. This sea does not have an outlet. It doesn't give freely of the water it receives from the Sea of Galilee. It literally hangs onto all the water and as the water evaporates in the hot sun, the solids in the water like salt stay behind. The sea is selfish and not charitable. As a result this sea is dead and it is literally called the Dead Sea.

The Sea of Galilee shares freely with its waters and life teems in its boundaries. The Dead Sea, on the other hand, hangs onto its water and there is very little life in its boundaries. Nature has a way of demonstrating the need for being charitable. If you are charitable, you will be filled with life and abundance. If you hoard and do not share with others, then you will constantly feel shortchanged and not have abundance. Your life will be barren like the great expanse of the moon or some desert where very little grows and life is scarce.

There are other examples in nature of the charitable spirit; one of the best is the flower.

Flowers are beautiful, as is noted in the book of Luke:

"Consider how the lilies grow. They do not labor or spin. Yet I tell you, not even Solomon in all his splendor was dressed like one of these."
—Luke 12:27

Flowers grow freely all over the world. They provide many things for us to enjoy and certain other animals to survive. In addition, flowers are the source for a great many perfumes and colognes. Flowers are beautiful and come in all kinds of shapes and sizes. Some provide food like the sunflower and others provide nectar for birds and insects like the dandelion and clover.

Bees live off nectar and pollen. The honeybee and bumblebee collect pollen into specialized sacks on their back legs. Bees also collect from nectar and make honey. Honey tastes differently based on which flower the bee harvested the nectar. From one of the most prized honeys is clover honey, which bees make from the clover flower. Birds, like the hummingbird, enjoy nectar and many have specialized bills or beaks adapted to certain types of flowers. They form a symbiotic relationship. In collecting the pollen and nectar, bees and birds provide a great service to the flowering plant by carrying pollen from one plant to another. Without this mechanism, it would be difficult, if not impossible, for the flowering plant to produce seeds and survive.

The flower gives freely to others and, in turn, ensures that it has life and passes it on to future generations. We are blessed that the flower shares its nectar with the honeybee, which in turn makes honey and stores it for the winter. The honeybee makes far more honey than it can consume and we share in the surplus. We, in turn, ensure the survival of the honeybee by building and caring for large numbers of beehives all over the world. When we are charitable with one another we increase the ability for all of us to survive and live full and abundant lives.

Flowers use an array of colors, shapes, and fragrances to lure in pollinators. This is why you will see brilliant colored flowers of all shapes and sizes. For instance, the honeybee does not see the color red, so you will not see a honeybee drawing nectar from a red rose. The red rose depends on the bumblebee. Some night blooming flowers depend on their fragrance to attract moths.

There are over 240,000 different types of flowering plants throughout the world. Those bearing "enclosed seeds" like apples and cherries are called angiosperms. Those bearing exposed seeds or "naked seeds" like pine cones are called gymnosperms. All these fruits and seeds start as a flower.

We depend heavily on flowering plants for our food. These include grains like oats, wheat, rice, corn, buckwheat, broccoli, and cauliflower. Think of all the seeds that we eat either raw or cooked in foods. Sunflower seeds and almonds are eaten raw, roasted, or made into candy bars. Other flowers provide dye or are used for their medicinal properties (e.g., roses, passionflower, prickly pear, and holly).

Some flowers are used to represent a particular meaning. If you send a dozen red roses, this is a signal of love. I once sent a dozen roses to a girl because I wanted to cheer her up. I was naive and didn't know the significance of the color of the flowers. She mistook this gesture as a signal that "love was in the air." How embarrassing! The proper color for friendship is yellow.

We send flowers to a funeral to show affection for the departed one and as a signal to the family that we care. When you travel to Hawaii, they greet you with a lei made of beautiful fresh flowers strung together with a string. They usually place this around your neck and greet you with a kiss. It's the Hawaiian way of welcoming you to their island paradise. Incidentally, Hawaii is blessed with some of the most beautiful flowers in the world.

Flowers are made up of four main parts: pistil, stamens, petals, and sepals.

- The pistil is the female part of the flower located in the center and contains one or more eggs, depending on the species. These eggs depend on pollen from other flowers in the same species in order to grow into little plants. This is why pollinators are so important.

- The stamens are the male portion of the plant where the pollen is produced. The pollen is located on long fibers that brush against pollinators, like birds and bees, when they are looking for food. These animals unwittingly carry the pollen to the next plant and fertilize the eggs.

- The petals are the leaf-like structures that we associate with the flower. They come in all kinds of shapes, colors, and sizes. Some of these petals are filled with pigments that are only visible in ultraviolet—bees can see them but we cannot.

- The sepals are the green structures that resemble leaves on the outermost portion of the flower. Their purpose is to protect the flower.

Each of these individual flower parts are referred to as whorls. Flowers that have all the parts are called complete flowers. Flowers lacking one or more of these parts are called imperfect flowers. This is how we get male and female plants. An example is the ginkgo tree. There are female trees whose flowers contain pistils but no stamens. The male tree's flowers have stamens but not pistils.

Flowers give away both pollen and nectar. They don't know whether any of the receivers of their gift will directly benefit them. I'm not implying that flowers think or sit and contemplate about this. I'm merely pointing out that their gifts to others have no strings attached. Over time, enough birds and bees carry enough pollen to other flowering plants of like kind to ensure their survival. Note that flowers give away nectar, which is expensive for them to produce and they also give away most of their pollen. What they get in return is abundant life.

So now that we have a good understanding of flowers and some of their potential uses, how can we apply the character of being charitable to our lives?

Let's first look at the two seas we talked about earlier. Are you the Sea of Galilee or are you the

Dead Sea? Be honest with yourself. It may be that you are charitable in some areas of your life and not in others. For example, you may give freely of your material possessions like money, food, clothing, et cetera; however you may be stingy with your time. This was the case with me. I found that I was open to giving things, but not my time. I often avoided visiting with people or spending any time with them because I had work to do. I finally realized that work will always be there, but some of the people I hold dear may not be. It was a hard lesson to learn.

If there are areas in your life where you are getting saltier, like the Dead Sea, and don't have a southern outlet, then figure out where you should put your southern river. Using the example I used earlier, I figured out I was stingy with my time, so I decided that I would make time for the people who are important to me. I have not been perfect at this, but I'm growing.

Make a list of those areas that you would like to be more charitable in. Then, think of how being charitable in those areas would benefit your life. Just as the flower gives nectar and pollen, it gets back far more than it gives. It gets a future generation and ensures its survival. The little things that we do for others can have a huge impact on our lives. Consider this passage from the book of Matthew:

> When the Son of Man comes in his glory, and all the angels with him, he will sit on his throne in heavenly glory. All the nations will be gathered before him, and he will separate the people one from another as a shepherd

separates the sheep from the goats. He will put the sheep on his right and the goats on his left.

Then the King will say to those on his right, "Come, you who are blessed by my Father; take your inheritance, the kingdom prepared for you since the creation of the world. For I was hungry and you gave me something to eat, I was thirsty and you gave me something to drink, I was a stranger and you invited me in, I needed clothes and you clothed me, I was sick and you looked after me, I was in prison and you came to visit me."

Then the righteous will answer him, "Lord, when did we see you hungry and feed you, or thirsty and give you something to drink? When did we see you a stranger and invite you in, or needing clothes and clothe you? When did we see you sick or in prison and go to visit you?"

The King will reply, "I tell you the truth, whatever you did for one of the least of these brothers of mine, you did for me."

Then he will say to those on his left, "Depart from me, you who are cursed, into the eternal fire prepared for the devil and his angels. For I was hungry and you gave me nothing to eat, I was thirsty and you gave me nothing to drink, I was a stranger and you did not invite me in, I needed clothes and you did not clothe me, I was sick and in prison and you did not look after me."

They also will answer, "Lord, when did we see you hungry or thirsty or a stranger or needing clothes or sick or in prison, and did not help you?"

He will reply, "I tell you the truth, whatever you did not do for one of the least of these, you did not do for me."

Then they will go away to eternal punishment, but the righteous to eternal life.

—Matthew 25:31-46

So like the flower, sow nectar and pollen and reap an abundant and eternal life. Give freely to the pollinators in your life. Remember that pollinators take on all kinds of forms. It may be a total stranger, a dear friend, or even an enemy. Just as the flower is pollinated by the bird, the moth, and the bee, we too, have our spirits pollinated by having a charitable heart. The seeds we produce will produce fruit far beyond our wildest expectations.

Consider the flower blooming in the meadow,
Advertising its generosity,
With beautiful colors aglow.
It gives freely, to those who have the need,
This is one of nature's lessons,
That we should take heed.

Chapter 11

Patience of
a Glacier

Count it all joy when you fall into various trials,
knowing that the testing of your faith produces
patience. But let patience have its perfect work, that
you may be perfect and complete, lacking nothing.
James 1:2-4

Patience often conjures up someone or something that is long-suffering, meets setbacks with a smile and encouragement, and is calm under the most trying of circumstances. Patience is what is needed to produce a fine sculpture or an engaging novel. It is a necessary virtue in climbing mountains or waiting for a plant to grow. The Japanese cultivate plants in miniature (bonsai) that literally take years to reach perfection. Patience is a young gymnast that wants to compete in the Olympics years in the future and must endure long and grueling training to perfect their skill enough to be able to compete. Patience is a virtue that is necessary to achieve the largest goals and the most difficult dreams. Without patience we will live stunted, unhappy, and unfulfilled lives.

Here are some great quotations concerning the virtue of patience:

"The key to everything is patience. You get the chicken by hatching the egg, not by smashing it open."
—*Arnold H. Glasgow*

"He that can have patience can have what he will."
—*Benjamin Franklin*

"Many a man thinks he is patient when, in reality, he is indifferent."
—*B. C. Forbes*

"Patience is something you admire in the driver behind you, but not in one ahead."
—*Bill Mcglashen*

"There are times when God asks nothing of his children except silence, patience and tears."
—*C. S. Robinson*

"Patience will achieve more than force."
—*Edmund Burke*

"Nothing great is created suddenly, any more than a bunch of grapes or a fig. If you tell me that you desire a fig. I answer you that there must be time. Let it first blossom, then bear fruit, then ripen."
—*Epictetus*

"Who ever is out of patience is out of possession of their soul."
—*Francis Bacon*

"Never think that God's delays are God's denials.
Hold on; Hold fast; Hold out. Patience is genius."
—*Georges-Louis Leclerc Buffon*

"All things come round to him who will but wait."
—*Henry Wadsworth Longfellow*

"Every man must patiently bide his time. He must
wait not in listless idleness but in constant, steady,
cheerful endeavors, always willing and fulfilling
and accomplishing his task, that when the occasion
comes he may be equal to the occasion."
—*Henry Wadsworth Longfellow*

"Slow and steady wins the race."
—*Aesop*

The Hare and the Tortoise

The Hare was once boasting of his speed before
the other animals.
"I have never yet been beaten," said he,
"when I put forth my full speed.
I challenge anyone here to race with me."
The Tortoise said quietly,
"I accept your challenge."
"That is a good joke," said the Hare.
"I could dance round you all the way."
"Keep your boasting 'till you've beaten,"
answered the Tortoise.
"Shall we race?"
So a course was fixed and
a start was made.

The Hare darted almost out of sight at once,
but soon stopped and, to show his
contempt for the Tortoise, lay down to have a nap.
The Tortoise plodded on and plodded on, and
when the Hare awoke from his nap, he saw
the Tortoise just near the winning-post and
could not run up in time to save the race.
Then said the Tortoise:
"Plodding wins the race."

There are many things in nature that we can
draw on for examples of patience, like watching
coral grow, waiting for a sea cucumber to travel one
foot, or waiting for a three-toed sloth to shimmy
down a tree. The sloth actually moves so slowly that
moss grows on its fur. All of these are good examples
of patience; however a better example exists in the
glacier.

Glaciers are an interesting phenomenon in
nature resulting from thousands of years of accumulation of ice and snow. These glaciers can be over a
mile thick and weigh so much that they actually
depress the earth's crust. A good example is the
glacier on the continent of Antarctica. This glacier is
over fourteen thousand feet thick and covers an area
of five million square miles. It's so heavy it has
crushed the continent and pushed it below sea level
in some places.

It is estimated that nearly 80 percent of the
earth's fresh water is trapped in glaciers and if it
were to melt, the oceans would rise by more than
200 feet. These glaciers are classified into three cate-

gories by the location where they exist: alpine—mountain glaciers, valley—glaciers that reside in valleys, and piedmont—lobe-shaped glaciers forming from one or more valley glaciers that spill out of a confined valley.

Glaciers move by sliding and by spreading out under their own weight. The best example I've heard to describe this movement is to take a spoon of honey and pour it on a plate. Notice how it moves slowly outward in all directions. The colder the honey, the more slowly it moves. This is representative of a valley glacier. Now slowly lift the plate on one side to simulate the steepness of the terrain. The steeper the incline the more this simulates the alpine glacier.

Over the years, these great chunks of frozen water begin to move, destroying everything in their path. They sometimes only move a few inches a years; however they can grind great boulders to sand. In their slow moving quest to the ocean, they carve great canyons and level small mountains.

Glaciers sculpt the land like a grand Leonardo De Vinci taking care to remove small amounts of earth to reveal a terrestrial *David*. In Glacier National Park, a combination of tectonic plates and glacial ice work together to create spectacular beauty like a potter working with a lump of clay to create a masterpiece. In Alaska, where the glaciers meet the ocean, great chunks of ice and snow fall into the ocean creating large waves and a popular tourist attraction. In one location, a great chunk of icy glacier fell into a channel creating a huge wave that washed away a great section of forest. A witness to this rare event was nearly killed by the wave. Even in its final death throws the glacier can still reshape the land.

Glaciers never get in a hurry. In fact, except in places like Alaska, where great chunks of ice regularly fall into the ocean, it is difficult to see any glacial movement. Yet slowly and methodically, glaciers make their way to lakes and oceans. And just as the tortoise beat the hare by methodically and patiently running the race, so too, does the glacier create spectacular canyons, lakes, and landscapes by methodically and patiently making its way to the sea.

The melting water from the glaciers creates streams and lakes that team with all kinds of birds, fish, and other animals. The pulverized soil becomes a fertile home for all types of trees, grasses, and other plants. The creative power of the glacier comes from gravity and the slow accumulation of snow.

We have much to learn from the glacier. The glacier never gets in a hurry and the changes often come so slowly that it is difficult for the human eye to discern; however the persistence and continual effort of the glacier is rewarded.

We live in a society today that expects instant gratification. Fast food, pay-per-view movies, credit cards, and even our medical field promises immediate cures by simply swallowing a few pills. Commercials create and solve problems in thirty to sixty seconds. We are promised instant weight loss by swallowing pills or surgery (liposuction), or overnight financial success by playing the lottery.

The deepest relationships, filled with love, do not happen overnight. They are the culmination of a thousand little things done over a period of time.

Financial success rarely occurs overnight. In fact, most lottery winners are broke within five years of winning. Just as it takes time for a glacier to pummel a boulder into sand, so too, does it take time to develop the discipline to become a good financial steward.

Healthy weight loss is not the result of swallowing pills or surgery. It is the result of a lifestyle change. It comes from eating a healthy well-balanced diet, supplementation (vitamins and minerals), and a good exercise program.

There are rarely short cuts in life. Anything worth having or achieving is worth spending the time to accomplish.

What areas in your life do you need to be more like a glacier? In my case, it has taken some time to create this book. I wanted it to go faster. Ultimately, I had to have a great deal of patience to complete it. Consider someone who wishes to become a medical doctor. They must prepare themselves for an extended amount of effort. Typically it takes four years to get their bachelor's degree and then an additional four years in medical school. This is followed by another three years as an intern. In all, it takes eleven years to become a doctor. It may take years to actually perfect this skill.

Take some time and study up on the glacier. There are glaciers on all the continents except Australia. Go visit a glacial site and look at the rocks that have been carved by these slow moving giants. If you are unable to travel to a glacier, consult an encyclopedia or look them up on the internet. Read the passages at the beginning of this chapter. You will lack nothing if you can make patience part of your life.

The glacier, God's chisel that shapes the land,
Creates beauty and wonder,
When held in His mighty hand.
Patience is our tool,
We wield in much the same way,
Carving a successful life by using it every day.

Chapter 12

Music and the Mockingbird

My heart is steadfast, oh God; I will sing
and make music with all my soul.
Psalm 108:1

Without music, our lives would be filled with silence or even worse, noise. Music tames the savage beast, or so the saying goes. When you say music, what comes to mind? Is it the melodious sounds of an Italian opera or the raspy metallic tunes of a hard rock band? Both fall in the realm that we call music and yet bring entirely different pictures to mind. Both are enjoyed by their audiences and few enjoy both at the same time.

Music is defined as: the science or art of incorporating intelligible combinations of tones into composition having structure and continuity or vocal or instrumental sounds having rhythm, melody, or harmony. What a mouthful. This definition, while accurate, does little to help us understand music. Music is beauty that is not seen with the eye, but heard with the ear, experienced with the mind, and felt with the heart.

Man has created all sorts of instruments for musical enjoyment; they range from the common guitar and piano to the exotic Chinese Erhu (two-stringed violin) and Indian sitar (an instrument that has from seven to twenty strings). We have managed to make music using common household items like the jug, broomstick, and washboard and our hands. Music is born in the soul of man and comes out in all forms like the beautiful sonatas from Beethoven and Mozart. Even poetry has a certain rhythm and musical quality. Ancient and primitive cultures were very rich in music and they regularly used instruments, dancing, chants, and singing during their ceremonies. Music has served as a form of worship to God, as a vehicle to communicate love, as a way to tell a story, and a method to enhance learning (i.e., like learning the alphabet).

Perhaps the most beautiful instrument is the human voice. Pictures of heaven nearly always include angels singing to God. My wife and I some years back took a trip to Hawaii and flew directly to Oahu from Atlanta. When we boarded the plane, we noticed a large number of women on the plane. After the plane got off the ground and both of us were trying to take a nap, the whole plane erupted into song. We were sharing a flight with the over three hundred singers from the quartet group called the Sweet Adelines. They sang for the entire eight-hour trip. It was very good; however we had difficulty getting sleep.

Music is the soul of beauty—it's the unseen breath of God which manifests itself in all sorts of places. Music can be heard in the croaking frogs on a spring night in the country. The frogs croak out their love songs to attract a mate. Crickets and katydids join the band of frogs to add the alto section of the group. The band is rounded out with an occasional hoot of the great horned owl or the yapping of a pack of coyotes. The evening, though dark with the exception of a few twinkling stars, is filled with the beauty of nature's ready-made band. The day time brings its own band of singers. Birds of all varieties chirp, cheap, whistle, warble, cluck, quack, and sing out their tunes for anyone to hear. Some songs, such as the screech of an eagle, bring terror to mice and voles, but sets the stage for a perfect summer day against a blue sky—much like a painting that comes to life.

Perhaps the most beautiful songbird is the mockingbird. The somewhat plain looking bird (not as colorful as a cardinal or indigo bunting) has one of the most captivating songs of any bird. The mockingbird mimics the songs of many other birds and sings its heart out for our pleasure. The mockingbird appears to enjoy itself by singing constantly. Because the mockingbird can sing so many songs (more than thirty), I call it nature's jukebox. Music is an expression of art and no bird symbolizes this better than the mockingbird. The bird paints a beautiful mural, using its voice as a paintbrush and the surroundings as its canvas. With each stroke of its voice, it clothes and blankets the land with sweet melodies. It expresses itself every moment that it sings. It weaves a tapestry of sound that lives for the moment.

These tunes are created by God. So, in a way, the mockingbird is a small sampling of the music we will all share in the great hereafter. If you have ever shopped for music on the internet, you might have noticed that you get to sample the songs on a CD (compact disc) before you buy it. Most of the time, at least in my case, I already have heard the song before I buy it. I'm usually surprised to find other songs on the CD that I like even better than the one that I originally purchased the CD to hear. The mockingbird is a prelude to better music to come.

Mockingbirds use their ability to mimic other birds as a defense mechanism to fool predators. The mimicry is so good that some birds of other species can't tell the difference. One such species is the red-winged blackbird. They live around ponds, lakes, and other bodies of water. It can also mock other creatures like crickets and frogs and some have even been known to mock manmade sounds.

Mockingbirds use their songs to attract mates and to ward off intruders. They have their own songs in addition to all that they copy from other birds. These unique songs are what they use to communicate to each other. Before we get into what we can learn from the mockingbird, let's take a closer look at how they live.

Mockingbirds eat insects, seeds, and berries. Their diet includes some of the following: ants, grasshoppers, spiders, beetles, blackberries, raspberries, dogwood berries, mulberries, elderberries, cedar, creeper, and others.

They are found throughout the United States, except for the upper western portion. They have grayish backs with lighter breasts and have a long bill. You can go to a number of Web sites on the internet and search for "mockingbird pictures" or go to a library and look them up in an encyclopedia to see what they look like.

Mockingbirds are territorial and are fierce defenders of their turf. They readily run off other birds that try to dominate them. Examples of some of the "bully" birds are blue jays, blackbirds, and starlings. The female mockingbird will defend her nest furiously against predators like snakes, hawks, and even humans if we try to get too close. This behavior is different than other birds.

I was walking through the woods on our farm one afternoon when I noticed what I thought was an injured turkey. I stopped and watched her for a moment as she fluttered back and forth in front of me with an outstretched wing. The wing looked like it was broken, however this hen was not trying to get away as I expected her to do. I remembered years earlier that a quail had done the same thing to me and at that time the quail was not injured but was trying to get me away from her nest. So as the turkey flopped around in front of me, I looked down in the grass and there all around me were little chicks. How I managed to walk into the middle of them without stepping on any still amazes me today. I carefully stepped back out of the nesting area and walked away. The hen immediately quit feigning her injury and went back to her brood. I wished I had a camera to capture the moment.

The mockingbird has been immortalized in poetry by poets such as Walt Whitman, Richard Henry Wilde, and others. It is the state bird of the following states: Tennessee, Texas, and Florida. There's even a movie called *To Kill a Mockingbird*, one of my favorite movies of all time, where Gregory Peck's character tells his son that when he was a little boy, his father admonished him to not shoot a mockingbird. I got the same advice from my father when I got my first BB gun. Thinking of a mockingbird as being a sample of the music yet to come in heaven should make us want to assist them in any way we can.

Do you have music in your life? If so, do you listen to music, sing, or play an instrument? If you are one of those talented people that have a gift for either singing or playing an instrument, then use your talent in the service of God. If you do not have musical talent, then let's look at some ways to add music to your life.

I'm not a very good singer, but I enjoy it. I love music and have a huge collection of CDs. I regularly make personalized music lists that have songs that either motivate me or cheer my spirit. You don't have to be musically gifted to make it part of your life. I believe God created us to enjoy music. We have been created in His image and He enjoys music.

Here are some thoughts about what type of music can make a positive input in your life:

- Avoid music that does not honor God.

- Avoid music that celebrates breaking the law or causing harm to others.

- Avoid music that does not honor you.

- Do listen to music or play an instrument every day.

- Sing at every opportunity (if you're embarrassed, sing in the woods or the shower)—it's good for the soul.

- Listen to different types of music (at least once)—you may be missing a real treasure (classical music and opera come to mind).

- Share your music with others—it will brighten their day.

If you live in an area where mockingbirds are abundant, take a stroll through the woods or neighborhood park and look for this wonderful creature. They will not be obvious from their calls—at least at first. Look for a bird that constantly changes songs. The best time to find them is in the daytime in the spring and summer. Look for areas where they will feed like mulberry trees or a thicket of blackberries.

Once you find a mockingbird, count how many different songs they sing. Can you identify the bird that they are mimicking? Sit back and close your eyes awhile and drink in all the sounds of other creatures in the woods or park. What do you feel? Is it peaceful? It is a glorious treasure to hear the sweet sounds of the mockingbird.

Music is a painting seen with your ear,
It fills your soul with happiness and cheer.
The mockingbird plays in God's heavenly band,
Playing music that is not just great—it's grand!

Chapter 13

Geese and Encouragement

But encourage one another daily, as long as it is called today, so that none of you may be hardened by sin's deceitfulness.
Hebrews 3:13

To encourage someone is to give confidence to them, hearten them, to cheer them on, persuade them, promote them, and push them. Encourage means to inspire with courage, spirit, and hope; to spur on and to help another achieve goals and objectives that are difficult to attain alone. Encouragement can often mean the difference between success and failure. Think of a sporting event where the stakes are high and the challenge is difficult.

For example, suppose that two fictitious teams are participating in a track and field event and the scores are close. The first team, let's call them the Cougars, have won most of their events and have a chance to be in the finals should they win the race. On the other hand, the second team, let's call the Falcons, have been undefeated and are assured of their place in the finals. As a result, the Falcons know they are going to be in the finals whether they win or lose. This is not the case with the Cougars. If the Cougars lose, they will not be in the finals. There is a single relay race left where whoever wins the race, wins the event. Let's further complicate the scenario by making the racers equal in the athletic ability.

As the race begins, the race is even and it stays this way through the first two runners. As the third leg begins, the fans for the Cougars know this is "do or die" and become very engaged in the race. They scream out encouragement to the runners and call them by name. They tell them that they have what it takes to win the race. The runners begin to find reserves that they didn't know they had. Little by little the Cougars begin to lead the race. As the race nears its final stretch, the Cougar fans become more excited and transfer their excitement to their comrades on the field. The runner pulls ahead and the Cougars win by more than two seconds, an eternity.

How could one team win so handily over another when they were so evenly matched? The answer is that the Cougars were motivated and drew their strength from the positive reinforcement of the surrounding crowd. Would they have won had there been no fans to cheer them on? Probably not. The power of encouragement cannot be underestimated or overstated. The Cougars had an advantage, even though they were not athletically better than the opposing team, the Falcons. Their advantage was a group of positive fans telling them they could win. Lack of encouragement is a major cause of failure.

While this story is fictional, this type of scenario plays itself out every day in the real world. Encouragement is always the deciding factor, all else being equal.

Most people think they can accomplish less than they are actually capable. They sell themselves short. How many dreams have died in the idea stage because they lacked encouragement? How many parents or teachers have destroyed a child's dreams by sowing discouraging words? Through encouragement we are able to achieve goals and dreams that we may otherwise avoid or never pursue. There are many examples in nature of the power of encouragement; the best example is Canadian geese.

Canadian geese mate for life and spend their summers in northern locations near water. They flock together and raise their families in a community that affords protection and camaraderie. Perhaps the best example of their ability to accomplish a difficult task is during the migratory season. Each fall the Canadian geese fly south to warmer climes that offer food and open water. These journeys can range from several hundred miles, to over a thousand miles or more. These long distances require a great deal of energy. A single goose flies in the lead position with others flying behind it on either the right and left sides. This formation makes it easier for the geese to fly by providing a slipstream for them to fly in with the exception of the lead goose. The lead must expend more energy because there is no slipstream for them.

A good way to experience the slipstream effect is by following a trailer truck. If you follow a truck from a distance, let's say one hundred yards or more, you will not notice any effect. As your car approaches the truck from behind, you will start to notice some buffeting and turbulence. If you get closer, just a few car lengths behind, you will notice that the buffeting decreases and it suddenly requires less energy to go at highway speed. You will actually be able to see the engine tachometer (instrument that indicates engine rpm—revolutions per minute) significantly decrease.

Unfortunately, this experiment is unsafe due to the reduced visibility that you will have, which will reduce the amount of time you have to respond to an emergency. Additionally, truck drivers are not fond of this because they can't see you and, therefore, it puts them at risk should they need to respond in an emergency.

Canadian geese can fly 30 percent farther by flying together than they could fly alone. This is great for the team; however what about the lead goose? They get no advantage of flying in a slipstream. Well, actually they do. The flock takes turns flying lead. If you watch a flock of geese flying south (or north in the spring), you will notice that occasionally the geese juggle location and a new goose moves into lead while the lead goose goes to the back of one of the legs of the "V" formation. While they're flying, you may also notice that the flock honks constantly. This honking is to encourage the lead goose who is working much harder than the rest. In goose talk, they encourage the lead goose to hang in there. The lead goose can't see his or her flock mates, however they can hear them.

By teaming up and encouraging each other they are able to fly long distances through storms, winds, rain, and snow. They have an instinctive goal to reach a warmer clime in the fall or to reach their breeding grounds in the spring. They are able to reach their goals because they surround themselves with others of like-mind that encourage them to excel. Imagine what might happen if the geese didn't encourage one another.

What if they didn't honk? What if the flock flew south in silence? Would they get to their destination? If they didn't make it to a warmer clime, would they find all the food they needed to survive the winter? In our lives, do we get all the encouragement we need to achieve our goals and fulfill our dreams? Do we encourage others to be all they can be?

What are some ways that we give and receive encouragement? First, encouragement can come from many different sources. We can read books that encourage us such as the Bible, *The Power of Positive Thinking* by Norman Vincent Peale, *Who Moved My Cheese* by Spencer Johnson, or *Think and Grow Rich* by Napoleon Hill. These books encourage us by painting a picture of what we could be and by challenging us to become a flower in God's garden.

We have so much to offer and yet often don't realize the full extent of our talents and the ability we have to live out our talents. We draw encouragement from others who have lived to their full potential, such as Moses, Jesus, Paul the apostle, Thomas Edison, Gandhi, Winston Churchill, George Washington, Benjamin Franklin, Disraeli, and many others. Their biographies speak volumes to those who have lived out their dreams and achieved their full potential.

We should avoid people and situations that are consistently negative. This does not mean that we should avoid criticism, especially when it comes from someone who wants you to achieve your best. This type of criticism is called constructive criticism and is a form of encouragement if done in the right way. As an example, suppose you are taking music lessons from someone who corrects you for not practicing and pushing yourself to get better. They still want you to achieve better results even if it is couched in the form of criticism (i.e., constructive criticism).

Negative people and negative situations can bring you down and delay or immobilize you from achieving your true potential. Negative situations can take on many forms from outright attacks on your abilities to the subtle approach, like a friend who talks you out of doing what you're capable of accomplishing because they are thinking of only themselves. An example of a friend (or someone who claims to be your friend) who works negatively, would be a situation where you are trying out for a sports team, band, or some other activity that allows you to fulfill your dreams and your friend discourages you from participating. They may tell you that you aren't good enough or that you may spend your time on the bench. It sounds like helpful advice to keep you from wasting your time; however the real reason may be that they don't want you to be occupied with other activities and have less time for them. This is a form of jealousy.

Sometimes encouragement comes for things we don't want to do. As an example, when I was growing up I had a strong mentor in my life. His name was Paul George Fiedler—most people called him P.G. He constantly pushed me to speak in public. I was literally terrified of standing in front of people. Yet he saw in me a talent for speaking and today, largely due to his persistence, I enjoy public speaking. His encouragement changed my life.

A true friend will always support you and demand that you excel, all the while cheering you on even when things look like you may fail. Seek others who encourage you to live your dreams. Do the same for others. Encouragement can be a kind word said to someone when they're having a rough day. It can be a cheer at a basketball game or a card sent to a friend just thanking them for listening. It can be a smile or a handshake congratulating someone for a job well done. It can be a hug given to someone you love or laughing with them in their joy. It can be a tear of sadness when someone is grieving or wink across the room to another looking for approval. It can be a beautiful bouquet of flowers or a helium balloon with "Have a nice day!" written on it. It can be an e-mail message with a famous quote or a smiley face written on the back of a napkin. It can be a prayer for their continued well-being or a cold soda on a hot summer day. It can be large, like a grant or scholarship to go to college and pursue your education, or it can be small, like putting in a good word at the local fast-food restaurant so that a deserving friend can get employment.

Take every opportunity to help others see the best in themselves. By encouraging others, you may well save a soul from a life of distress or mediocrity. You can literally change the world around you by being a positive force in other people's lives. And as you give freely of your encouragement, God will likewise fill your soul with peace and love. Like the geese, you will soon have your turn to be in the lead and you will need others to spur you on.

Encouragement is the energy we give and receive,
It helps us our full potential to perceive.
With the others to support us and cheer us on every day,
We will become flowers in God's garden on display.

Chapter 14

The Persistence of Salmon

*God will give to each person according to what
he has done. To those who by persistence in doing
good seek glory, honor, and immortality,
he will give eternal life.*
Romans 2:6-7

Persistence is based on the word persist, which means to go on resolutely or stubbornly in spite of opposition. A good example of persistence is Thomas Edison, who literally tried thousands of combinations of filaments in order to make a workable electric light. In spite of failure upon failure, he persisted in his dream of making a workable incandescent lightbulb which could dramatically change our world. Thomas Edison and his assistants tried over six thousand different vegetable fibers and it wasn't until he stumbled across using carbon as a filament before he could get a lightbulb to burn long enough to be practical.

"I never failed once. It just happened to be
a 2000-step process."
—*Thomas Edison*

"Persistence is to the character of man as carbon
is to steel."
—*Napoleon Hill*

"Energy and persistence conquer all things."
—*Benjamin Franklin*

"Nothing in this world can take the place of persistence. Talent will not; nothing is more common than
unsuccessful people with talent. Genius will not;
unrewarded genius is almost a proverb. Education
will not; the world is full of educated derelicts.
Persistence and determination alone are omnipo-
tent. The slogan 'press on' has solved and always
will solve the problems of the human race."
—*Calvin Coolidge*

"Winners are losers who got up and gave it one
more try."
—*Dennis DeYoung*

"Fall seven times. Stand up eight."
—*Japanese proverb*

"People may fail many times, but they become failures only when they begin to blame someone else."
—*Unknown*

"The most essential factor is persistence—the
determination never to allow your energy or enthu-
siasm to be dampened by the discouragement that
must inevitably come."
—*James Whitcomb Riley*

"A jug fills drop by drop."
—*Buddha*

"My son, observe the postage stamp! Its usefulness depends upon its ability to stick to one thing until it gets there."
—*Henry Wheeler Shaw*

"One of the most difficult things everyone has to learn is that for your entire life you must keep fighting and adjusting if you hope to survive. No matter who you are or what your position is you must keep fighting for whatever it is you desire to achieve."
—*George Allen*

"Let me tell you the secret that has led me to my goal: my strength lies solely in my tenacity."
—*Louis Pasteur*

Persistence was necessary for George Washington and his troops during the Revolutionary War. The British were superior in nearly every way on the battlefield and Washington lost nearly every battle. Yet with all this against him, he still ultimately led his troops to victory and helped create the United States. The British lost their resolve to fight—they were not dedicated to their goal of keeping their empire intact. The colonists, on the other hand, were dedicated to separation and self-rule. They were dedicated to creating a country where the laws were decided by the people being ruled. They were persistent in this belief and triumphed as a result of it.

During the mid 1950s and throughout the 1960s, the United States and the former Soviet Union were in a space race. Each country was competing for world domination in technology and space. The Soviets were the first to put a satellite in space. On October 4, 1957, the Soviets succeeded in launching Sputnik. The United States followed on January 31, 1958, with Explorer I. The Soviets were the first to put a man in space when Yuri Gagarin was launched in April 1961 aboard Vostok 1. Again in June 1963 the Soviets launched the first woman (Valentina Tereshkova) into space aboard the Vostok 6.

To make matters worse, the United States was conducting their space program in the eyes of the public while the Soviet Union conducted theirs in secrecy. The world saw the rockets in The United States blow up on the launching pad. They never saw any failures from the Soviet space program (though there were many). Yet through all this, the United States stayed the course. It was persistent. As a result of this persistence, the United States was the first to put men on the moon on July 20, 1969, when Neil Armstrong and Edwin Aldrin walked on the lunar surface.

Many astronauts died throughout the space program and many mistakes were made that took years to overcome. Persistence and an attitude that failure was not an option, allowed the United States to reach its goal.

Are there any examples of persistence in nature? Yes, there are many, however the salmon is one of the best examples. Perhaps no other creature is more persistent than the salmon. Salmon have been known to travel hundreds (sometimes thousands) of miles from open ocean waters, up rivers and streams to spawning grounds far inland. Along the way they don't eat, face all kinds of predators, swim up waterfalls, and ultimately die of exhaustion. All of this so that they can lay eggs and make sure the next generation has a chance. Many salmon species, like sockeye, lay their eggs in fresh water, but live their adult lives in the salty waters of the open ocean. They then return to their old stomping grounds to lay eggs in the fresh waters of a mountain stream or river.

Pacific salmon start their life as alevin, a stage where they live off their yolk sacs. They graduate to small-fry living in the cool waters of a stream or river. They feed on insects and water plants, and as they grow they take on different colors and markings. Typical markings include dark stripes; at this stage they are called brandlings. As they continue to grow, they become bright silver and begin their migration to the ocean. At this stage, they are referred to as smolt (about two years old). There are several kinds of Pacific salmon, such as sockeye, coho, pink, chum, and chinook and each has its own color scheme.

The salmon grow to maturity in the open blue waters, often very far from land (hundreds of miles). They will remain in the ocean from one to seven years depending on species. There they feed on smaller fish like herring and krill.

When the salmon reach the spawning stage, the male undergoes physical changes. The snout becomes longer and hooked, the dorsal fin gets a fleshy lump, and their heads turn green. The female undergoes some changes too, but they're more subtle. Her abdomen swells (because of the eggs inside her), her jaws only slightly elongate, and her head turns green. Otherwise, she maintains her silvery color.

At this point, the salmon migrate back to their place of birth. They join up in large schools and become easy targets for predators of all kinds. Once they reach the inlet to the river or stream where they are going, they cease eating and their bodies turn red. Many of the rivers and streams that the salmon traverse are filled with all kinds of obstacles like waterfalls, shallows, fallen logs, and rapids. Along their difficult path they face bears, eagles, raccoons, otters, and other land predators. Many die from exhaustion or are killed by disease resulting from their bruised and battered bodies hitting rocks and skimming gravel.

At last, they make it to the spawning grounds and lay their eggs in the gravel. After they finish spawning, they die. Their bodies litter the streams and are soon eaten by vultures, bears, opossums, and other animals that eat carrion. In these shallow streams the whole process starts over again.

Not once during their trying ordeal does a salmon quit because it's too hard. They face dangers during their entire trip and yet never waver from their goal. Many die in the pursuit of their quest to reach the place where they started their lives. No obstacle, no problem, or no amount of difficulty would stop them short of death. This is persistence!

How can we apply the lessons of the salmon to our lives? Do you have goals that you have not met because you did not stick with it? Are they true goals?

When I was about twelve years old, I wanted to play basketball (or at least I thought I did). I had several friends who had joined the team and I didn't want to be left out so I joined too. My parents were not all that keen for me to play basketball and at the time I didn't understand why. It was a ten mile drive through the country to my school and my dad refused to make the trip (this was before the age of the soccer mom). He told me that if I wanted to play, I had to find my own way home.

The first practice it took me nearly an hour to get home because I had to walk and hitchhike. After a couple of times of this, I quit and never played basketball again as an organized school sport. My parents knew that I wanted to be on the basketball team for the wrong reasons, so they put some obstacles in my way to allow me to make the best decision. It worked.

I wanted to play basketball for the wrong reasons and so was not persistent in the pursuit of that goal. Incidentally, a few years later I joined the football team and faced a similar dilemma in that I needed a ride to and from school. This time I had joined the team for the right reasons—because I wanted to play football and because I liked exercise. I never missed a practice and was never late. I was persistent and enjoyed sports as a result.

When we embark on a goal or objective, we will inevitably encounter obstacles. How we respond to these obstacles is the key to our success. If we quit or settle for a smaller dream, then we do not live up to our full potential.

I admire, as I think most people do, those who overcome all kinds of obstacles and succeed anyway. Look at Helen Keller who was blind and deaf at birth. Yet despite these handicaps, went on to lead a full life and inspired countless others to do the same. Or consider Victor Fraukl, author of *Man's Search for Meaning,* who endured the Nazi camps during World War II. He survived and suffered some of the most horrendous torture while many around him gave up and died. He wanted to tell the story of the events that occurred in Dachau. He had a purpose that kept him alive. Because of his persistence in getting through each day, we can read about the atrocities that these prisoners endured. His story shines as a beacon to others to persist when everything around them looks hopeless.

We can learn from the salmon. In spite of everything that is thrown in their path, they persist to their goal—even if it costs them their lives.

As always, seek divine guidance through prayer and then stay with it like the salmon run the rivers and streams. When you meet some of life's waterfalls or log jams, jump them and keep going. The race goes to the persistent.

❧

Salmon are persistent as they traverse the river,
They go on against adversity until they die in a quiver,
Leaving behind a future generation in the rocky brook,
God's example of persistence is there, if we only look.

Epilogue

As we have seen, nature has much to teach us about the way we live and govern our lives. We need only open our eyes and allow our senses to experience the wonders that God has created. In this book, we covered fourteen character lessons which have grouped into four categories as follows:

- Dealing with others
- Physical health
- Growth and expression
- Personal character traits

The chapters that are grouped into the category of dealing with others are *Flowers Are Charitable, Geese and Encouragement, Dogs and Loyalty, Eagles and Teamwork,* and *Family Life of Honeybees.* In these lessons we learned key character lessons that, if applied, can dramatically improve our lives and the lives of those around us.

The chapters that are grouped into the category of physical health are *Horses Like to Run* and *Bears Need Rest.* In these two chapters we learned the valuable lessons of exercise and rest and the key role they play in our lives.

The chapters that are grouped into the category of growth and expression are *Spiders and Creativity, Music and the Mockingbird, Otters Have Fun, and Trees Seek Out the Light.* In these chapters we learned lessons that help us grow and use our talents to enjoy life and to express ourselves.

The chapters that are grouped into the category of personal character traits are *The Persistence of Salmon, Ants and the Work Ethic,* and *Patience of a Glacier.* In these chapters we learned lessons that help us develop our personal character by observing the world around us.

By enjoying your surroundings and allowing God to instruct you through His creation, you can become all that He has planned for you to be. Beauty and wonder are literally in your backyard. Pray for guidance and your eyes will be opened to lessons from the world around us.

If you have individual stories to share concerning nature, please let me know. I appreciate all feedback.

Author Contact Information

By U.S. Mail:
P.O. Box 50
Hamburg, IL 62045

Phone: (866) 536-5485
E-mail: <u>dennis@natureslessons.com</u>

www.ingramcontent.com/pod-product-compliance
Ingram Content Group UK Ltd.
Pitfield, Milton Keynes, MK11 3LW, UK
UKHW020813120325
456141UK00001B/74